# The Wonder of Christmas

Jeanne Conte

# The Wonder of Christmas

## Jeanne Conte

*Jeanne Conte*
*Merry Christmas!*

ThomasMore®
~Bringing Faith to Life~

Allen, Texas

Scripture taken from the Holy Bible, New International Version, Copyright © 1973, 1978, 1984 by International Bible Society. Used by permission.

Photo Credits: © The Crosiers/Gene Plaisted, OSC, pp. 18, 46-47, 60-61, 82, 102-103, 108; Jeanne Conte, pp. 6, 64, 80.
Cover Design: Desktop Miracles
Text Design : Tricia Legault, Kristy Howard

COPYRIGHT © 2001 by Jeanne Conte
All rights reserved. No part of this book shall be reproduced or transmitted in any form or by any means, electronic or mechanical, including photocopying, recording, or by any information or retrieval system, without written permission from the publisher.

Send all inquiries to:
Thomas More Publishing
200 East Bethany Drive
Allen, Texas 75002-3804

To order additional copies:
Telephone: 877-275-4725 / 972-390-6300

Fax: 800-688-8356 / 972-390-6560

Visit us at: **www.thomasmore.com**

Customer Service E-mail: **cservice@rcl-enterprises.com**

Printed in the United States of America

Library of Congress Control Number: 2001092521

**7477**   ISBN 0-88347-477-8

1 2 3 4 5     05 04 03 02 01

*For to us a child is born,
to us a son is given,
and the government
shall be on his shoulders
and he will be called
Wonderful Counselor,
Mighty God,
Everlasting Father,
Prince of Peace.*

—Isaiah 9:6

*(written about 700 years before
the birth of the Christ-Child)*

# Contents

| | |
|---|---|
| Introduction | 9 |
| The Legend of the Star-of-Bethlehem | 11 |
| Little Jesus | 19 |
| A Wonderful Christmas | 21 |
| lamb of the Lamb | 29 |
| Jacob's World | 31 |
| The Gifts | 35 |
| Wallpaper World | 47 |
| Silent, Stille Night | 53 |
| The Christmas Coat | 57 |
| A Recent Bethlehem Christmas | 60 |
| A Broken Christmas | 65 |
| Eduardo's Homecoming | 71 |
| The Yule Fire | 77 |
| The Legend of the Holly | 80 |
| The Little Shepherd | 82 |
| The Crimson Christmas Ribbon | 85 |
| The Petticoat of Heaven | 88 |
| Stranded in a Snowstorm | 95 |
| Out of Egypt I Called My Son | 103 |
| Listen! Christmas Angels | 109 |
| A Birthday Party for Jesus | 115 |
| Acknowledgments | 128 |

# Introduction

There is a wonder to Christmas that words cannot touch. It is beyond words, "It is below and in front of and behind—this wonder that is of Christmas."

Isaiah said that "his name shall be called 'Wonderful, . . . .'" And, indeed, the story of this Christ-Child is the beginning of wonder to those who hear and would believe; and it is the whole of wonder if, after believing, one attempts to comprehend; and it is the continuing for all time of this wonder if, after all, the story is true as has been believed for hundreds of years by millions of people.

This wonder speaks of a love described by poet Christina Rossetti as:

> *Love came down at Christmas,*
> *Love all lovely, Love divine;*
> *Love was born at Christmas,*
> *Star and angels gave the sign.*

In the following collection of Christmas writings, I have only, in my poor way, tried to allude to this love and cast a glimmer of the reflection of this wonder that is above all others—the wonder that is Christmas.

To go straight to the story is too much for one to take in and too much for me to ever tell. But if one would try, it has been written, and it is there for all who would read it in the sacred writings of He who is the author of life and love and Christmas itself.

# The Legend of the Star-of-Bethlehem

The hardy and tender bulbous plant, *Ornithologalum Umbellatum*, commonly called the Star-of-Bethlehem, forms a starry white carpet of flowers in early summer. It is a member of the lily family, *Liliacaea*. Its flowers form perfect six-petaled stars. It is said that it exists to remind us of the real star of Bethlehem and that the reason it has no fragrance is because the fragrance was given as a gift to the Holy Child that night in Bethlehem.

Jared heard the story from the neighbor shepherds and ached to see the wonder of what they told. It was such a marvel, and though only ten years of age, he planned to make the journey to Bethlehem, the City of David, to see the baby they called Christ the Lord. He had two friends, old Moab and Jonathan, to accompany him. Together they packed parcels of food for the journey.

He heard that real angels sang "Glory to God in the highest and on earth, peace to men of good will," and "Tidings of great joy!" All this ran through Jared's head as he wrapped his meager pack—an old sheepskin to keep him warm (his only change of clothes), some goat cheese and dates, flat bread, water, and the few coins he had saved.

Hey, we must hurry! How long would they stay, the young couple and the baby Christ?" Perhaps now that they were leaving. Jared nudged the others with anxious motions and soon they were on the road—the sometimes dangerous road, but the road that led to the City of David and the baby "wrapped in swaddling clothes, lying in a manger" as the other shepherds told them.

These three, each with his pack and his shepherd's crook for a stave and with glaring sun overhead, dug their sandled feet into the hot desert sands enroute to Bethlehem.

"Moab."

"Yes, Jared?"

"What did they mean—'The glory of the Lord shone round about them.' Moab, what did they mean"?

"I wish I knew exactly, young Jared. I can only imagine as you. One said that it was like a glorious light with beautiful heavenly music and that there was a host of angels."

"Host? What's a host, Moab"? Jared asked.

"Oh, Jared," joined Jonathan, "You know, a lot . . . a whole lot."

"Like the sky full of them"? came Jared.

"Yes, boys, they said the sky was suddenly filled with singing angels, but only after one spoke to them. But what fantastic words!"

They talked that day as they walked, those three, and it was exciting. Moab, though up in years, was seasoned with daily work and carried his age well, only holding them back a little. He was their guide, as he had been Jared's guide through the years, since he had been without family. Moab found a job for Jared and gave him a corner in his tent. It wasn't much, but it was a place for him to sleep.

Jared wakened in his corner when the shepherds came rushing in that night with the great news about the Christ-Child. The neighbor shepherds were loud and excited, but Moab was quiet and serious. Jared listened late into the night, wide awake with wonder. When they all left it was near daybreak. Jared straightened the tent, firing questions at the quiet old man who stared straight ahead, deep in thought. That was a few hours ago and now the lack of sleep, the travel, the excitement and the wonder, greater than any of them had known in all their days, left them very tired.

They knew they must find a place to rest for the night. Other than a gnarled old olive tree, they could find no shelter and water. The heat of the desert took its toll on their small supply. The darkness offered respite from the sun but the desert turned cold at night. Although they were fearful of animals, they dared not make a fire that might attract thieves known to travel the area. So they lay close together on their backs examining the stars so white and one so magnificent against the blackness of the night.

"It's so beautiful, the sky, all blue and white by day and now . . ." Jared's words failed him. The beauty of that night was like none other and his heart was so full. His eyes glistened like the very stars and his throat was so filled with attempted description no word could escape.

Quietly, old Moab responded: "He gives you this because He loves you."

Now Jared's throat gave way to choking tears, but not like those when his mother died. He didn't understand why and Jonathan did not understand why, but old Moab knew and reached his hand to Jared's and held it fast, until the tears were spent and exhaustion claimed them and they slept, those three, beneath the old olive tree.

Jared woke suddenly to the sound and smell of horses. He reached for Moab but only found Jonathan sitting bolt upright, his fists rubbing his eyes. Then he saw the horses behind him with three men on them, one leaning over with his huge whip raised high, about to strike old Moab. They'd already taken the packs and staves, and old Moab was holding tightly to Jared's water cask when they struck.

"Stop! Oh, no! No!" Jared ran toward them as Moab fell and the black-cloaked bandits leaned forward, kicked their horses which kicked showers of sand in their getaway. They disappeared into the desert from whence they had come. Then all was quiet as if they had never been there. Only, they had been there and they left death.

Jared, weeping, lifted Moab's head into his lap. Moab never opened his eyes. He, too, was gone, as Jared's mother and father had gone. A long time passed before Jared turned to look at Jonathan.

His hands nervously clenching and unclenching, Jonathan sat in the scant shade of the tree.

"We must bury him and go home," Jonathan said. "There is no water."

Jared looked back at his water cask, still clutched in Moab's hand. The water made a dark pattern on the sand.

Together they buried the old shepherd under the olive tree, and the young shepherds urgently debated what to do.

"We're half way there, Jonathan. We're still alive. God spared us," Jared reasoned.

"We've lost everything—our food, water, money, and our guide. We'll die too, Jared. We must try to make it back," Jonathan answered.

Jared solemnly sunk his sandals into the sand and shook his head. "I'm going to see the baby—the Savior King."

So the two shepherds shook hands and Jared stood by the grave of the old shepherd in the shade of the old olive tree and watched his friend, and only companion, walk away from the sun. He watched until he could see no more of him—only the shimmering that divided the sky from the sand.

Jared's throat was full now, but this time also with the swelling from dryness. He looked to where his water cask spilled and in its place a tiny flower bloomed as if smiling in the scrub weed of the sand. Jared knelt and looked closely at the beauty of that tiny starlike flower that pushed itself up from the wetness here in the middle of the great desert and, again, he thought he had never seen such beauty. Then he remembered what old Moab said about the beauty of the sky:

"He gives you this because He loves you."

Jared's tears mercifully moistened his throat as he gently scooped up the still moist sand and flower, wrapping then in his old sheepskin against the desert heat. The young shepherd then turned into the sun and continued toward Bethlehem.

The sun blazed overhead; his body agonized for water; Jared staggered slowly onward. He didn't even know that when he fell forward onto the soft welcoming sand, he had lapsed into unconsciousness.

He awoke this time to the taste of cool water poured across his parched lips. He drank eagerly, then opened his eyes to such a sight! A king on a camel wearing a royal crown and silken robes smiled down at him as his camel handler lifted Jared carefully.

"Oh please! My flower!" Jared struggled eagerly down and opened his sheepskin to see it still fresh and beautiful in its sandy pocket. Now it was the king and his men who gazed in wonder at that desert miracle. Jared grinned. "He gives you this because He loves you," he said.

"He what?" the camel handler stammered. But the king raised his hand for silence and looked intently into Jared's eyes.

"Where are you going in the desert with that flower, little boy?" asked the king.

"To see the Child—the one the shepherds saw in Bethlehem."

(A solemn silence)

"Then you shall come with us. Would you like to help with the camels when you are feeling better? We have also come a long way to see the Child. You don't look too well right now. So you may ride with me on my camel.

Now, tell me all about how you came to be in the middle of the vast desert and how you came to know about the Child."

The king gazed tenderly at the small boy who looked for all the world like the son he'd never had and for whom he'd often yearned. Surely this finding of the boy with his flower in the barren desert was a sign from the great God. His faith had been tested by seemingly endless days of desert travel. The others in the entourage smiled their approval as they began moving forward again toward the great star.

That night, when the star settled over the stable, the kings knelt in wonder and splendor at that which was above all splendor. The very air itself seemed radiant as Jared peeked from behind his kingly escort.

The Holy Family looked down at the magnificent array of gold and frankincense and myrrh. And there on the edge of this kingly display nestled a very small flower, its scent mingling with the fragrant spices. The mother smiled as she touched it, murmuring, "Little star—star of Bethlehem."

Much later, as the royal group began its long homeward journey, Jared nestled on the camel's saddle in the king's arms.

"But why, . . . who . . . who is this wonderful child, sir"?

"His gift to us, because He loves us."

# Little Jesus

*Little baby,
come to be living here
on earth, like me.
You, the Son of God on high,
in a little manger lie.*

*Little God-Child
will you be ever close
and near to me?
You, come down from heaven above
just to share your great, sweet love.*

*Little Gift
from heaven above—
little Jesus,
made of love.
You, the son of God on high,
in a little manger lie.*

*Little Jesus
from above—
little Jesus,
you I love.
You, the son of God on high,
come to earth to live and die.*

# A Wonderful Christmas

*"Good tidings of great joy. . . ."*
Luke 2:10

I am lying on my stomach, snuggled on my pallet under deep, quilt mounds in my grandparents' attic. My cousins lie nearby. It is Christmas Eve and the magic is here. Wind-driven rain pounds hard at the attic window as we gaze, mesmerized, into the liquid night, straining hard to hear the slightest tinkle of sleigh bells.

It is a dormitory, this attic, for my cousins and me each Christmas. It is high and we can stand tall under its steep-peaked eaves. A long clothesline is strung down its middle where sheets hang from clothespins—all in a row—the divider between the boy and the girl cousins. Away from the clean-swept middle of the attic where our rows of pallets lie—all along where the roof lowers—ancient-to-us trunks and mysterious boxes hug the edges.

But the happenings of the moment fill our minds and whispers spread like a warm, sweet haze, hovering and moving among my cousins and me on this most wonderful of nights.

And among the wonders of this night comes one so totally unexpected! The much admired cousin next to me whispers a secret in my ear.

"Promise you won't tell," she says in all her seriousness, and I promise, eager to be let in on something so important by this exalted person.

"You are my favorite cousin." I can hardly believe and am astonished at the thought! "I like you even better than...."

It is with amazement and wonder that I, the awkward, gangly one who never knew quite what to say, was so esteemed and as I stammered a thank-you, I pondered the thought. This will be my best present ever this year, I am sure—to be so valued and accepted—and placed first in the eyes of this accomplished one.

I try hard to sleep (knowing that the sooner I fall asleep the quicker the morning comes), and I envision the pretty scene downstairs.

The tree stands tall, all the way to the ceiling and it is wide-spreading and decorated with tinsel and bright-colored balls. Silver icicles hang carefully, one by one all over the tree, falling long and reflecting in a myriad of ways the colors of the tree lights. Cotton snow surrounds its base, barely covering the white sheet peeking out here and there, as if wishing to join the festivities.

And there, under the tall tree, under its wide-spreading branches rests the subject of the celebration—the tiny baby Jesus with arms outstretched, too, as if welcoming and condoning this warm, treasure ritual of the observance of his birthday.

Around him there are the presents, such small, human semblances in memory of the great gift—Jesus. These are wrapped in various colorful designs or in red or white tissue paper with bright bowed ribbons.

These are the gifts of the drawing and that is a year-long thing filled with secrets and wondering, this drawing. But gifts from Santa Claus will come during the night—mounded around and spilling over our socks hung during the Great

Depression so each of the drawing gifts are bought dearly or fashioned by hand. It spreads the fun secrets over twelve long months, and allows that much time to tuck a few coins away now and then to finally make the purchase —all the while wondering and trying to figure out the perfect gift to be purchased with Depression-time money.

It is especially fun during the year when we visit grandmother's house and watch her as she crochets this or that or hooks a rug or sews on the machine—always creating something—but for whom does this one go or that one and there is always this wondering and happy guessing. Smiles—secret smiles and spying a wrapped package tucked high on a closet shelf.

I found a private way of figuring out some of the gifts— the magazines. I looked through them, these wonderful women's magazines stacked high on the sun porch. There were coupons clipped from copies of *Ladies Home Journal*, *Women's Home Companion*, and *Good Housekeeping*. And I found in one kitchen drawer a great collection of box tops—but for what and for whom?

I am still awake. It is Christmas Eve, and everybody around me now is fast asleep. Finally, my body begins to give in but it must be near dawn. No one is to go downstairs before 6:00 A.M., and no one is to wake up anybody else. I finally fall asleep and, instantly, there is all this raucous! The boys are whooping, the girls are stretching and grabbing their bathrobes, and I hear mother's voice on the stairs:

"Good m-o-r-n-i-n-g. It's C-h-r-i-s-t-m-a-s!"

We tumble downstairs and, as some of us line up for the

bathroom, others group into the grandparents' dressing closet or bedroom, jerking arms through sweaters and legs through long stockings and we quickly appear in our finest clothes.

The rule is well-known. No one enters the Christmas tree area—the living room—until the grandparents say so. And that is after we're dressed and all have finished breakfast.

Tables are set in long rows in the great grandmother kitchen, made up of boards laid across sawhorses made by grandfather, and topped with clean, white tablecloths, nicely set.

We are finally assembled and grandfather reads from the Bible the story of the birth of Jesus, and he asks the blessing and we begin. Our spoons delve into hot oatmeal and it takes so long to finish even with warm, melted brown sugar oozing all around the milk in our bowls. We have to wait politely until everyone is through . . . sitting, fidgeting . . . with smiles cracking our faces—on and off—and then, . . . we are ready!

"Walk, not run. . . ." But it is useless. We tear into the big room and there are the socks we gave grandmother—the largest each of us had, and they aren't hanging up anymore, but heavy with fruit, candy and nuts, and a few secrets stuffed within. They lay in a row on the floor, and there are other things alongside—treasured gifts guessed and unguessed, asked for and unasked for—but nothing, of course, very expensive; it is the Depression.

I spill my sock on the floor, catching the round, shiny hard candies with fantastically beautiful centers—each a little different, and I pop one into my mouth as I look. There is a big orange stuck in the toe, and three large red apples, pecans, walnuts, hazelnuts, and a Brazil nut. And I have an embroidered handkerchief and a doll trunk for my Shirley Temple doll. But best of all is the white bunny fur muff, the one in the store window I was sure I could never have!

I become aware of talking and tune my mind back to everyone else. We are asked to join our individual families for the gift exchange, so we gather our socks and their contents and sit around the big room on the floor by our parents, and everyone sits quietly waiting for grandmother to appoint one of us to distribute the gifts—the gift-exchange gifts!

We open them one by one, and it is done nicely, not all in a frenzy like with the socks. I love grandmother's! She has crocheted dresses for my Shirley Temple doll and they fit into the doll trunk. I watch, staring closely at the faces as the gifts I brought are opened, and I worry lest they aren't liked, but they are liked. I can tell.

Then, we're hurriedly snuggled into coats and scarves (many with new ones), and I stuff my hands into my new white bunny fur muff and it's into our cars and off to the church—the strange, different church of the grandparents. The music swells, rising and lowering and surrounding us with the most joyful sound I've ever heard, and I sit enthralled and entranced and hear again the story of how God gave us the baby Jesus.

Then it's back to the grandparents' great, warm house where we cousins play and talk, while our mothers stir around the kitchen. Wonderful smells waft through the house, melding with the happiness and exchange of talk and playing of new games and examining of new toys. A boy cousin got a tape recorder and he hides it here and there, guffawing when we catch him at it.

An aunt sits at the piano and Christmas hymns float through the room, and, after a time of enjoyment and leisure, we girls are called to help grandmother set the table or chop carrots for the salad or stuff cheese into celery. We carry heaping bowls full of tasty food, quickly while still hot, into the dining room.

The big table is long and beautiful and soon heavy with food, and we children have our own table with the sawhorses underneath. We sidle around, saving places for favorites, and me—for the cousin who said I was her favorite of all. Everyone comes to dinner, and grandfather says grace again, but this one is special and long and good and thanks God for the great gift of his loving son and his grace and kindness and all of the gifts and food and for each other and for all of us being there together.

And I think—I wonder what is this word "grace" and I promise myself to ask later. But now it is the fine dinner and we delight in it, and we talk and it is all warmth and happiness. If it could only last, if it could only go on and on, I think.

In the afternoon, after the table is cleared and the dishes done, we play with our toys some more, till Mother makes us take a rest. In the quiet of the rest time, I lay on the cool enclosed sun porch, snuggled in a quilt, thinking of all that has happened.

Then it is the time. Each year there is always the time when "Scrooge" is scheduled on the radio, and we never miss it; it is so much a part of my childhood Christmas. We all gather around for that, and we listen again to the story wondering how anyone could ever be a Scrooge.

Afterward, I ask my all-knowing grandfather full of

wisdom, "What is this word, grace"? And he says:

"It is something given to someone who doesn't deserve it." And I wonder and ask if he is talking about the Christmas presents and which ones of us don't deserve them, and he answers:

"It is the great gift—the love-gift of Jesus coming down to earth as a little baby at Christmastime to live and to die for us, even though none of us could ever, ever deserve such a gift." That is "grace." And I tuck it into my mind, to think on many times. I know that there is someone who loves me always, because of this thing called "grace."

The Christmas is tapering off and cousins, one by one, pack their bags and leave into the cold outside air. They leave in cars with my aunts and uncles driving to their far-away homes. We are filled with this wonder, still, of the story of the birth of this child of God sent down to us from heaven and the Spirit of it enfolds us in its amazing warmth.

As another much-esteemed older cousin is called to her car, she runs back to me and gives me a surprise hug and whispers also in my ear those never-before-this-Christmas-heard words:

"I don't want anyone else to know—they might get their feelings hurt, you know,—but you are my favorite cousin. I just had to tell you!"

She squeezed my arm, and with the nicest smile I'd ever seen, she drifted away into her parents' car and the greater outside world, and I was left to feel that there will be Christmases again, and I will look forward to them all year long, each and every year. But there can *never, ever* be another Christmas as wonderful as this.

# *lamb of the Lamb*

*Sleep on, O lamb of the Lamb, sleep on;*
    *and may his angels guard, protect you,*
    *with their shimmering wings enfold you,*
    *tenderly love, tenderly hold you;*
*O lamb of the Lamb of God, sleep on.*

*Dream on, O lamb of the Lamb, dream on.*
*Dream of the Christ-Child's heavenly birthday,*
    *presents, toys, love and child play—*
    *happy people all through that day;*
*O lamb of the Lamb of God, dream on.*

*Sleep on, O lamb of the Lamb, sleep on;*
    *and when it comes that you must wake*
    *and grow to manhood, don't forsake*
    *all he'd ask of your life to make.*
*But for now, O little lamb, sleep on.*

# Jacob's World

*Life is the childhood of our immortality.*
—Goethe

How like the Madonna and Child they looked! And with the father hovering about, one had the feeling of Joseph, too. Radiant, all of them. A joy-filled time, the coming of a newborn into the world.

"Do you want to hold him?" they asked. Before I, in my hesitation, could answer, they deposited tiny infant Jacob into my uneasy arms. This miracle of newness of life, this wonder of creation. This just-born being lay softly, gently—sensing.

I could sense his sensing. We sensed each other. Eyes alert, it was as if every fiber of his being felt the world he had just entered.

There are those who "have a way" with babies, who can soothe the crying ones just with the confident way they pick them up and relate to them. I am not so gifted. When my own children cried, I cried, too. When they agonized, I agonized. Although I loved them dearly, it was not simple for me, this rearing of children.

So I sat still, waiting for this newborn infant to cry. But he didn't. He looked earnestly at me while lying quite still in my awkward arms. He must have listened to my heartbeat, smelled the soap I use, felt the warmth of my body and sensed safety in my embrace. His life could have depended on that and, somehow, I am sure he knew.

We sat together silently for a long while before someone gently lifted him from my arms, passing him around to others of our admiring family.

The weeks that followed offered opportunities to be with this little fellow. Although, there were times when his happiness was beyond my control. For the most part we got on quite well.

Once, after little Jacob had an especially fussy day, my daughter needed me to baby-sit. When she got home, I honestly said that he was just fine.

"But what did you do?" she asked.

"Well, he showed me all the toys in his crib for one thing," I answered.

"He did?" she puzzled. (Jacob was one month old.)

"Well, yes." And I recalled how he, with his eyes, looked at each toy, and how, on this cue, I picked them up one by one, examining each closely. Jacob's eyes moved on to toy after toy, until we examined them all.

Not long after that, my daughter again asked me to baby-sit awhile so she could do a little gardening. That's when I noticed her peeking around corners to see what Jacob and I were doing.

"How Jacob loves his rubber ducky!" I grinned as she caught us lying on the floor where I held the duck overhead and made it squeak while making sporadic sweeping motions down toward a delighted Jacob.

We shared lots of similar games, Jacob and I—the old peek-a-boo and the disappearing blanket. When all else failed, I let him pull my hair. We built a relationship.

I sometimes wondered, as I slipped in and out of visits with my daughter's young family, how Mary's mother Ann might have experienced her role in the lives of Mary and Joseph with the baby Jesus.

The thought came to me that God continually gives us this mirror—this thought-provoking reflection of his own entry into our world on earth. He, who always offers us hope and new beginnings, demonstrates the miracle of newness of life and hope through his gifts of tiny babies.

Christmas arrived when Jacob was nine months old, and we wondered how he might react to the evening of our family's traditional gift exchange.

In the middle of the room, where we all sat around laughing, chatting and smiling, ripping paper and tossing ribbons and bows, sharing in happiness and giving and warmth, Jacob stopped in his eager crawl, turned his head, looked over his shoulder and caught my eye. Grinning at me, he raised his head just a little, while emitting abrupt, happy "Ah!" sounds. I replied in turn, and, for what must have been several minutes from our separate places across the crowded room, we related in our own way, in our own world, framed by living joy.

This was the first celebration of the Christ-Child's birthday in Jacob's world.

# The Gifts

They watched with growing worry their mother's pain. When it was bad (which was too often, lately) she walked a little crookedly, hesitating on her right leg as if she didn't want to let anything touch the left one. And when she had to walk, her face was set in that way with her lips in a straight line. She had little money so they did not have much—except her love and that was wonderfully boundless, extending as high and wide as the great western sky arching grandly and beautifully over them all.

It was a good thing for they lived apart from the town—out a way—so they had to be each other's company, but good company they were. After their father died, their mother had to sell off the land, bit by bit, but they held tight to their home, hoping to keep it, living on as little as possible, and yet finding many ways to have fun and be happy.

Amy-Anne Alysia told her brother Rowan Alexander that their mother must have thought hard to give them such elaborate names as if that was the one thing she was able to do for them. No one in their entire school had names like theirs.

Rowan Alexander and Amy-Anne Alysia did what they could for their poor mother because her love for them was so sweet their own reflected right back. They didn't have to be told to pick up their clothes or straighten their rooms.

In fact, they straightened up the other rooms and laid out their Mother's afghan on the big soft chair and started dinner for her every day.

They loved to see her smile and hold out her arms to them and tell them they were the best children in the world, and then she would look toward the big window at the sky and her face lit up in this soft warmth of hers and she would whisper (as if they couldn't hear), "Thank you God!"

But the sand-filled autumn winds changed to wintry blasts and their little Thanksgiving chicken dinner was long past. Christmas was coming and although they knew full well the true meaning and it filled them all with joy, Amy-Anne Alysia and Rowan Alexander and their mother each longed to be able to give each other some very special present to show their love.

"I have an idea," Rowan Alexander said to his sister one day as he looked in the hall closet, spying his Mom's old ukulele on the top shelf. "Let's make a song for her."

"A song!" Amy-Anne Alysia replied, a frown on her face. "How in the world can we do that?"

They had seen pictures of their mother with that ukulele in her arms from when she was a teenager, but she seldom played it anymore. In the days when she did play it, they watched and remembered, and now Rowan Alexander stood on a chair and gingerly took it into his own arms, holding carefully to the back of the chair as he stepped down. Amy-Anne Alysia watched in awe as he placed it under his right arm and began strumming it with his fingers.

Suddenly Amy-Anne Alysia remembered where the book was that told how to play and she even found the old tuning fork. Before long, they were singing "We Wish You a Merry Christmas" with not-too-bad accompaniment.

"O.K," Rowan Alexander said as he rested his hand by his side, still holding the old instrument. "Now let's think up a song just for Mom—a present for her."

Amy-Anne Alysia beamed. They had less than an hour before she would be home, and how they worked. Nothing sounded quite right, but the idea was there.

A frown furrowed Clair's forehead during her long ride home on the bus. If only she had enough money—just enough to give Amy-Anne Alysia and Rowan Alexander really special Christmas presents. But today she was given notice. Before Christmas she would receive her last pay check, and it would be so very hard to find another. How would she pay the bills? How long could the little money she had last—how long could they keep their little house? Fear gnawed at her heart.

"My goodness!" she murmured, not realizing she had said it aloud, and the other riders turned and stared at her. Clair looked out the window at the big azure-blue sky and prayed silently awhile. Then a thought entered her mind, and in spite of all, a smile crept over her face.

"Hello, Mom!" Amy-Anne Alysia and Rowan Alexander greeted Clair at the door and for a long moment they held each other in a warm embrace. Somehow, Clair's arms were always wide enough to hold both her children tightly and she loved the smell of them—the rough wool of Rowan Alexander's sweater and the shampoo in Amy-

Anne Alysia's silky soft hair that fell like an auburn cape over her slender shoulders.

The meatloaf also smelled good. But how could she tell them about the job? She decided to wait until after Christmas. Why say it? It wouldn't really help. They already knew money was very tight and they didn't complain. They were such blessings! Clair nuzzled her head into the two of them and made a little growl sound and said: "Umm! I could just eat you up, I love you so!"

Laughing, the youngsters pulled away, and asked if they could start making paper chains after dinner to decorate for Christmas, and Clair brightened at the idea. "I've some old catalogues I've saved and we could cut colorful strips from them and make flour-water paste. Let's do it! And we can make popcorn, too!"

So the evening went on without a trace of Clair's new worry. In fact, it was as if they all were especially happy. But in the back of her mind, Clair was thinking of where she might apply for a sit-down job, as her leg would not allow her to stand for any length of time. When she said good night with kisses all around, she said she thought she would read the paper awhile in bed.

Clair turned the thermostat down quite low after seeing that Amy-Anne Alysia and Rowan Alexander had extra covers on their beds. Snuggling under her own thin blanket with her coat laid on top, Clair read carefully each employment ad, realizing she should stop the paper tomorrow and read it at the library. Then she laid it aside and thought about what she had decided to give her children for Christmas. The frown worry left, a smile crept in, and Clair turned over to begin her prayers. She had no job. She had so little money, but she felt a deep happiness.

"I give it to You, Lord," she prayed. "You know that I have done all I can think of to do. I know You love us. I thank you for your bountiful blessings, and especially my children and Your Child Jesus. Please take care of us." Clair soon fell sound asleep.

The next day after school, Amy-Anne Alysia and Rowan Alexander struggled with ideas for their song.

"It has to be chipper—up and happy," declared Rowan Alexander.

"I think Mom would rather have something soft and sweet," Amy-Anne Alysia replied.

"On a ukulele?" came Rowan Alexander. And on it went.

They took turns strumming and humming and ideas surfaced, were weighed and partially or wholly rejected. But they were becoming more proficient, and in the evenings the room filled more and more with cheerful, colorful chains, and the happy secrets made for furtive smiles and camaraderie. The warmth and joy that only comes with Christmas filled the house in spite of the pain, chronic lack of money and material things—and hovering job loss.

Clair left the house at her usual time each day, but not for her old job. She made the rounds of job applications, then spent time in the library studying ads. She often stopped at a church to kneel in silence asking God to help her find a way to care for her children. Then she returned home at her usual time. The children suspected nothing.

Christmas Eve came sooner than seemed possible, as the anticipation was such a pleasant thing. Amy-Anne Alysia and Rowan Alexander could hardly hold back their secret, but they were finally ready, having compromised with a series of sweet, soft verses followed by a snappy, though lyrical, chorus. They had practiced until it flowed quite well, in spite of how Rowan Alexander's voice had the frustrating and embarrassing habit of changing just when he was hitting an especially high note. They even worked out a way of singing in harmony during the chorus, with Amy-Anne Alysia singing in her soft alto voice complimenting Rowan Alexander's spirited tenor.

They had a very small tree set on a table glowing with hand-made ornaments, one long popcorn chain, and numerous diminutive paper chains matching the larger ones encircling the room. Mom made her famous fudge but only a small batch, so this year it was saved for Christmas day.

"But we can each have one piece before bed on Christmas Eve, don't you think?" Mom said in her especially sly way of talking, just barely hiding the smile that fought to break out.

"Sure!" came the shouted reply.

So after a special pancake supper with a chopped apple and a few chocolate chips thrown into the batter, lathered with butter and syrup on top, they played dominoes for a while. Then Mom asked for the Bible and Rowan Alexander brought it to her as she sat cuddled in her afghan in her soft chair. She read the Christmas story from St. Luke and then she passed the Bible around. Amy-Anne Alysia looked up a passage about Christmas in another part of the bible, reading it aloud; Rowan Alexander did the same.

Then Mom asked them to bring the fudge which had been placed on Mom's prettiest plate. Smilingly, they savored their pieces, carefully placing the rest into the refrigerator for Christmas Day.

Although it was quite late, they were terribly excited and it was hard to fall asleep. Rowan Alexander kept peeking into Amy-Anne Alysia's room to whisper that he had the ukulele under his bed and that they would bring it out together and even though it was cold, they would tell Mom to put on her coat so they could sing their song to her outside under the great western sky that arched lovingly overhead.

A few tears of happiness slipped onto Clair's pillowcase as she thanked God for her children and for sending His own Child to earth.

"Merry Christmas! Wake up, Mom!" It was morning so soon. Clair grinned widely and grasped her children in that familiar hug, squeezing extra hard today.

"Merry Christmas yourselves! Shall we have breakfast or our presents first?

"Presents!" They exclaimed in unison.

"Mom, we have a special surprise for you. But you have to put on your coat first," said Amy-Anne as she pulled Clair's winter coat from atop of her bed and began thrusting her arms into it's sleeves. Clair wondered what in the world they had in mind. Such a cold day! Outside at dawn? But this worked right into her own plan, so she grinned and "obeyed."

Rowan Alexander brought in a tray with three steaming mugs of hot chocolate. He gave it to Amy-Anne to take outside with them. The he left the room briefly, coming back with one arm held secretively behind.

"My what a wide grin you have!" Clair teased as they opened the front door to the most marvelous sunrise imaginable! The sun was just peeking above the far-away horizon, as if nudging away wide glorious strips of color—pink, orange, magenta and lilac. A few scattered stars glittered around the western part of the sky, as some high serras clouds rippled high above—a masterpiece of magnificent beauty.

They all stood looking for some time, then Rowan Alexander nudged Amy-Anne Alysia and they took their pose with the little sister sitting on the edge of the porch step while the elder brother stood beside her, one foot on the step beside her and the ukulele resting on his bent leg. They began their song, softly at first:

*Far away in Bethlehem
the little Baby came to be—
Hope for all eternity,
yes, Mom, for you and me.*

*And in that stable far away
little Baby Jesus lay;
this King from Heaven—a tiny Child
asleep upon the hay.*

*No matter what will happen here
He'll care and see and know;*

*and may He always be with you*
*everywhere you go.*

*A long way off in Bethlehem*
*He came from Heaven above,*
*He came to bring us all, dear Mom*
*His sweet and gentle love.*

*He gave us our vast western sky*
*He gives His loving care;*
*He made it all from His great love;*
*He's with us everywhere.*

*No matter what will happen here*
*He'll care and see and know;*
*and may He always be with you*
*everywhere you go.*

Clair's eyes were wet, yet wide with wonder; her heart ached with joy. Their gift echoed her own. Suddenly her arms were around them again; she showered them with kisses, thanking them and showing her awesome pride.

"You are so good!! Where did you learn all that? How did you do this?! Well, honeys, thank you from the bottom of my heart!"

Then she began slowly, softly at first.

I wondered and wondered what I could possibly give you that would in any way show my love. Then I thought, God gives to us so bountifully. He has given so much to me. I want to give to you—I want to give you—(now don't laugh)—the sky—the great forever-sky. God gave it to me and I have always loved it, so now I give it to you. Our western sky goes on forever. When we stand tall in our western prairies, we can look in all directions for hundreds of miles, and when we look at the sky it is the grandest thing in the world to see. Like this morning with the sunrise and with its myriad clouds flying across and at night the zillions of stars. It brings the rain to cool us, the breezes that refresh us, the storms that entrance us and tell us of His power, the sun to warm us and allow us light. I give you our forever sky and want you to remember that it will go with you everywhere you go and be your constant companion and no piece of art in any gallery can ever compare with its beauty. And somewhere up there I believe your God is watching over you and me and that somewhere up there, we will spend eternity. For this Christmas, I give you this—this thought. And always, after I am gone and whenever we are apart, look at that sky and remember me.

Rowan Alexander and Amy-Anne Alysia listened intently, smiles wreathing their faces.

After a sumptuous Christmas breakfast and another taste of fudge, Clair told them to sit down as she had another present to share.

"Our great, good God does indeed answer our prayers! I lost my job a month ago, but while praying about it in a downtown church while you were at school, the pastor asked if he could be of help in any way and after I shared with him my story, he offered me a job as his receptionist. And, guess what, this job offers benefits and so I may be able to get some surgery eventually to help my leg pain. And tomorrow, we'll go buy you each a set of new clothes!"

As they rode to Christmas services held in Clair's new church, Rowan Alexander's and Amy-Anne Alysia's eyes stared constantly out the window at the vast forever sky—theirs to keep (as if it wasn't always—but now in a very personal way). It arched over them in loving embrace, deep blue with the whitest imaginable fluffy clouds racing along in the winter wind over the western prairies.

# Wallpaper World

It is the sameness that is so unbearable. Each gray day like a string of cheap beads—all the same dull, lusterless color and size, strung out interminably.

We are all old, here, and growing older and it is as if we are the forgotten generation—surely the unwanted one. I refuse to live from one bland meal to the next. The pains of arthritic joints and rheumatic flesh grow daily into the most interminable burden. I gaze at a single flower on the papered wall and dream my dreams.

Now the wallpaper flower becomes many and I gather them, admiring each bloom, savoring its scent—its velvety texture—marveling at its exquisite beauty.

"Emily, stop!" My mother's memory voice. I'm caught. The flowers are forbidden touch-me-nots and I come back from my wallpaper world.

I look absently at the row of rocking chairs across the bleak parlour, each with its aging occupant. Above them is strung a Christmas garland over the top of a row of windows, winding down at one end as if to indicate the tinseled tree in the corner. Under it are small packages, each individually wrapped in cheap paper. We'll each receive identical "gifts" of talc or cologne or the like.

I want to scream at the futility and boredom, but, instead, squeeze back self-pitying tears.

"What's the matter, Miz Pardon?" It's an aide.

"Nothing. I'm all right." And I turn my face further away, concealing my wet eyes, abhorring intrusions in my pain-world.

I make no friends. Persons come and go here with frequency. Usually they arrive in frustration and hurt with cooing family members whose visits quickly fade into nothingness; leave via ambulance or, more often, hearse.

It is easier not to notice.

Now as I gaze at the wallpaper flower, I see the corsage William brought me for our first dance. The ribbon was light blue satin to match my gown and he stood with the celluloid box clutched in his scrubbed hands, his head ducked in embarrassment.

Next, the flower becomes a part of my wedding bouquet. As I toss it into the air, I fling myself into William's arms and feel his warmth and strength as the scent of the bouquet pales against his masculine cologne.

I hear my mother sobbing, and then come back to the present as I hear real sobbing in my real world. It is the person in the chair next to mine and it is a woman also blinking back tears as her shoulders heave in convulsive rhythm. As I turn to her, she winces and turns bodily away, echoing my own most recent movements and I suddenly feel deep empathy for this other person trapped in my wallpaper world.

My hand, without my willing it, reaches out to touch hers. But she pulls hers away quickly as tears stream down her unwilling face, and now she turns away further so that I can no longer see, intruding into her own pain-world.

Now my hand touches her shoulder and pats it consolingly. I feel her feel my touch and the feel is noticeable and it is as if I have anointed her with the balm of Gilead.

Her sobbing noticeably wanes, yet expends itself as if the outpouring is necessary to cleanse some deep wound.

We sit in silence a long time. Then she speaks.

"I saw in that wallpaper flower over there a remarkable similarity to the bouquets my husband sent to me in the hospitals when our children were born," she says, and I see her choke back more sobs.

I try a smile and she tries, too, as our eyes meet for the first time.

After a while, I speak.

"You know, when my husband passed away, I had a small corsage pinned inside his casket. The flower also reminds me of that."

From the corner of my eye, I see her steal a quick look at me, and then nod her head. Trays rattle and the aide comes to ours and notices they are not touched. She scolds as she carries them away.

Suddenly, I want to leave this stifling room.

"Would you like to go for a walk with me?" I find myself asking, and then, to my horror, I notice for the first time that she has no legs and her "chair" is on wheels.

But she smiles. She really smiles, and I find myself pushing her chair down the long corridor. I am in my coat and muffler now as I tuck a blanket around my friend and we somehow manage to get through the exterior door to the outside world of fresh, cool air.

Crystal snow sparkles in mounds forming a corridor through which we pass. Distant sounds of carolers drift across the clear cold air to us. Somehow, in spite of the cold, I don't feel my arthritis pain as severely, but dread the spasms this trip will bring.

My friend turns her head and calls over her shoulder:

"This is the first outing I've had in months!"

We see cars laden with weary shoppers inching their way through the holiday traffic, bundles piled high in rear seats and we see the look of warm anticipation on their faces.

We see how the snow clings to the north sides of tree trunks and branches, tracing lacy filigrees against the evening shadows. We look up and catch snowflakes on our faces. I extend my tongue and catch one and we both double up in laughter.

I pause to drink in the sweet stillness of the pristine snow blanket which quiets the world with its omnipresence. The difference between the constant din inside and this fairy world—a classic study in contrasts.

Now I am pushing the wheelchair past some children who are throwing snowballs and their rollicking laughter infects us. My friend turns in her chair again, grinning. I stop and scoop up enough for both of us and we test our marksmanship on a nearby fire hydrant.

"Are we ready to go back?" I ask, wondering about how much pain the cold will bring on in my legs.

"Sure. By the way, I notice your limp. Would a good massage help? My hands and arms are still good and I used to do that for my husband.

"Would it? My goodness, yes!" I marvel.

We sit, now, beside each other at Christmas Eve dinner. I feel better than I have felt for a long time; with the exercise and massage, my body actually seems to glow.

There are real fresh flowers beside our plates for this occasion. We open our gifts and find, instead of talc or cheap cologne, small Christmas angels.

# Silent, Stille Night

The battle raged
for days and days.
So tired! They grappled
through the haze.
Fight or die;
they struggled on,
unrelenting—
so forlorn.
Their buddies fell
in mud and mire,
victims of enemy fire.
Then a voice pierced through
the battle's roar.
It was the sergeant,
Charley Moore.
"Tomorrow, boys,
what do you say?
We'll ask for a truce
for Christmas Day"?
But how to ask
so they'd understand
in their language in
this foreign land?
It was too dark
to raise some white—

*a flag for truce
in the dark of night.
So, loudly, Sarge
began to sing
this Christmas carol's
familiar ring:
"Si-i-lent Night—
Ho-o-ly night."
Then joined the rest
(a lull in the fight)—
"All is calm,
All is bright."
Down the rows of men
in the sodden night
came the Christmas carol—
cheerful, bright.
The sounds of war
slowly stopped.
Soldier's gear
in the mud was dropped.
Even from
the enemy's side
no shots were fired—
no more died.
Echoing
the same holy song
the enemy sang—
a peaceful throng?
"Silent night, holy night,"
"Stille nacht, Heilige nacht,"*

"All is calm, all is bright,"
"Alles schlaft, einsam wacht,"
"Round yon virgin mother and child,"
"Nur das traute, hacht heilege paar,"
"Holy infant so tender and mild,"
"Holder knabe im lokkigen haar,"
"Sleep in heavenly peace!"
"Schlaff im himmlischer ruh!"
On they sang
through the dead night,
till morning dawned.
And in its light,
Charley looked
on his men who lay
in the mud and blood
by the light of day.
Then Charley knelt
by his men who slept—
never to waken—
and Charley wept.
But his buddies
heard him
say this prayer:
"Holy Child,
see them lying there?
It's Christmas Day;
I ask this prayer:
'May they sleep in heavenly peace—
sleep in heavenly peace.' "
Amen.

# The Christmas Coat

Jacque and I wrapped the small packets carefully, swathing each in colored cloth or paper. Then I tied them with bright ribbon. To some, the small packets weren't much, but they were very hard for us to gather together.

There was a small lump of real sugar, some hickory nuts, dates, and a small angel that Jacque carved from a block of wood and that I dressed in ribbons and lace from Mama's hat—the hat that Mama left behind when the troopers stormed the house and took her away.

Mama hadn't resisted like Papa had last year. He struggled, pleading that he had a family who needed him, but they shot him anyway and Mama buried him in the cellar, bathing the dark earth with her tears. There was just no one to come and bury him properly, but we each said prayers over him that day, and Mama said she was sure God heard every word and that he took Papa to heaven where he would be happy always.

Jacque and I hid in the cabinet with the feather covers when they came for Mama. She told us to do that if they ever came back. I think she went with them quickly so they wouldn't find us.

It is so hard to find food! Our neighbor lets us stay in her cellar, but she, too, is fearful and there is little to eat for anyone. At night, sometimes, Jacque and I come back to the house to prepare for Mama's Christmas.

We think they have her at the big prison that is not far from our house. There's barbed wire wound into a lumpy fence all around that place. Between this and the prison buildings, there is a wide stretch of ground where the prisoners are sometimes allowed to walk.

Jacque and I used Papa's spy glass to look for Mama, and we thought we saw her three times. Her hair wasn't curly anymore, and she looked sad and thin and cold. That's when we decided.

We planned to take her coat to her on Christmas day and stuff the pockets with little presents. Jacque cut strips of ribbon from my red skirt, and we used gold foil from the candy box that Papa gave Mama two years ago.

We figured it this way—I would put on Mama's coat, pinning up the bottom with safety pins and cuffing up the sleeves. Jacque would throw Papa's thin wool coat over the barbed wire and climb up to the top and tie on a rope. I'd climb up the knotted rope to the top; then we would switch the rope to the other side to let us down inside, and we'd run real fast to the building and find Mama.

We had it all figured out. You see, we'd rather be with Mama in the prison than out here alone just waiting to be caught and all the time hungry and scared and so lonesome for her.

Anyway, if we could find her, there is still the slim chance we could all get back out the way we got in. The place we chose was close to the woods, where it was not too hard to hide.

Now it is Christmas Eve and getting very dark, and it is time to go. We have been praying to the Christ-Child to be with us.

"Go with God!" Mama used to say to Papa when he left for work.

"Go with God!" I say to Jacque, and he smiles bravely back at me. He carries Papa's coat and the coiled rope, and we creep through the woods wishing the moon wasn't so bright.

We wait until the searchlight passes. Then Jacque quickly throws Papa's coat over the sharp barbs and climbs to the top. He ties the rope and throws it down to me, and I shinny up fast, my heart beating loud like a drum.

We drop inside into the deep snow, and Jacque grabs his leg. I see red blood from where a barb cut his hand drip a bright Christmas red onto the white snow.

"Run fast!" he whispers. "My leg is twisted. Go!" he orders.

I freeze, staring at Jacque's Christmas-red blood, thinking of Jesus' blood and my arms go around him.

The searchlight lands on Papa's coat and the rope, and there are shouts; then the searchlight is on us and machine guns roar.

But now there is this incredible peace. Instead of cold snow, the sun shines, bathing us in warmth. I see flowers growing higher than houses, and Jacque and I are floating upward with kites and balloons, and the kitten and dog we used to have are with us.

And I hear the angels, and I see Papa coming to greet us with his big, warm smile and his arms reaching out widely to us. And then Jacque cries, "Look! Mama's coming too!" And I look back and see her following us, smiling and all warm in her Christmas coat.

# A Recent Bethlehem Christmas

"But Mama, why?" Nadia wrenched the words between sobs. "I didn't do it. You didn't do it. None of us hurt anybody—Why do they take away our Christmas?"

The mother, whose arms were already full with a crying baby cradled in one arm and a fretful toddler clutching at her knee, drew Nadia into the warmth of her embrace. It seemed all she could offer. Her older children sat sullenly at the table set meagerly but festively for Christmas Eve. There were warm, round loaves of flat bread and dishes filled full of yellow hummus, lovingly decorated with paprika and olives.

But all celebrations were again canceled in Bethlehem. Green-garbed soldiers with rifles slung over their shoulders patrolled the area with heavily staffed check points near the Church of the Nativity. No one was allowed to enter. Traditional candle-lit processions, holiday Masses, and carol-singing were all canceled.

"But all we were going to do was pray for Papa and for the poor and ask God to hear our prayers as long as our candles were burning," Nadia's sister blurted. "It couldn't hurt anyone!"

"We can still do that," her mother answered softly.

The sister went on, as if she didn't hear, "In American movies, everyone has presents—many presents. Maybe someday I can go there."

Her brother's eyes blazed as he raised his fist toward her. "To America! How do you know their guns didn't kill grandpa and help take our land from us? You would go there?!"

"Shhh!" the mother tried to calm them. Her voice was soft so that they had to strain to listen. "There were guns from many places. And, do you think that all of those things—those many gifts—make them happy? Do they bring them close to God?"

She looked around at the frustrated, unhappy faces and continued. She hadn't planned these words. They surprised her as they fell from her mouth in this heated moment.

"We are suffering. But now, when I pray, I feel very close to God. He suffered so much that I know that he understands and cares."

"I wish Papa would come back," Nadia interrupted.

"Shut up, Nadia!" the tall brother jumped up from the table. "How do you think Mama feels?"

"Shhh," soothed the mother. "We'll all pray for Papa. We'll pray that they will treat him well. We'll pray they'll let him come home very soon!"

An Israeli guard had been killed. They rounded up ten Palestinians for questioning, and their father was one of them. It happened weeks ago, but there was no word of him. The father was innocent, but that was the way it was done. If no one confessed, many were punished.

"I hate them! I hate them! If they hurt Papa, . . ." and the tall boy again raised his fist into the air.

"Stop!" the mother's voice trembled. It is Christmas! Did Jesus hate? Did they hurt him? What did he say to do?" She is crying herself now. "It is hard. I know, my children. It is hard—but he gives me strength to go on and he'll give it to you, too. You must ask him. And—you must love."

"I cannot love them!" the son's dark eyes burned with frustration and a terrible feeling of helplessness.

The mother spoke again. Her voice was quiet. It was as if a blanket of soft quietness descended around the group.

"With God you can do anything, my darlings. Before all of this pain, I forgot about God. I was just interested in silly things that had no meaning. Now I talk to him all the time. If I didn't have him, I couldn't go on, and it is a wonderful feeling to be so close to him. You see, the suffering has done me good!" and she smiled.

The baby was quiet now and Nadia's sobs were gone. The mother rocked to and fro in a soothing way, enfolding three in her arms and beseeching the others with her eyes. They glistened as they looked from one to another, entreating them to come with her in this journey of understanding and love.

She looked at her eldest son. "You can carry the cross in place of your father and we'll have our own procession right here inside our house. Nadia, you can light the candles for your other brothers and sisters. See, I've saved them for tonight," and she opened a napkin to show a neat pile of candles, some used, but each carefully trimmed.

"But first," she said, "We'll pray. We'll pray for the poor like we always do at Christmas. And we'll pray for Papa, especially. But then we'll pray for everyone in the world who suffers, because now we understand that. And then we'll sit together and break these round soft loaves of bread and dip them into hummus and thank God that he gives us this food to eat even without a father to care for us."

They all held hands around the table as their mother led the prayers. It was as if a peace came upon them all and a closeness they had never known. When the mother finished the last "Our Father," Nadia lit the candles for the procession. Then the tall son reached for the crucifix, but it was gone.

Then, in the shadow of the doorway, he saw the figure of his father. Even in the darkness, one could see the bruises, but his face had a look of gladness about it that was as if he had seen angels. And in his hands he held the crucifix.

"Merry Christmas, my beloved family!"

And there was a joy then that passed understanding and that this family had never ever before known and which was a gift—the greatest gift to them, this closeness to God and to each other.

# A Broken Christmas

If they were only there for me. Parents! Frustration gnawed at his inner being like a rat at a hunk of cheese. Josh delivered the last pizza, mechanically accepted the small tip and headed home. A myriad of colors—neon lights interwoven with commercial Christmas decorations—reflected on the slick, wet pavement, as he skidded to a stop at a traffic light.

Josh sat there, his windshield wipers mechanically clicking. He was lost in thought. If only he could cope better, somehow, with his many heaped-up problems. He was wishing someone understood. "I could deal with it all better if Dad or Mom were just there for me," he thought. "How I wish they really cared—would just take the time to sincerely ask how I am and act as if I mattered to them."

Thoughts came crowding in, but solutions eluded him. There was Tony the class ringleader who constantly ridiculed him for not doing drugs. There was the impossibility of understanding calculus, yet Josh's Dad was an engineer. There was Jill who seemed to like him, and he liked her, but she always refused when he asked her for a date. And the track tryouts were coming up and he knew several of his competitors used illegal stimulants. If only. . . .

The honking of horns shocked Josh into the present as he gunned his engine, spun his wheels and lurched into an uncontrollable spin across the intersection.

A sudden crash and intense pain was the last thing Josh remembered before awaking to the antiseptic smell of an emergency room.

"Just relax, son." A pair of steel gray eyes between a blue cotton hat and mask looked down on him.

"I'm not your son," Josh thought as he tried to sit up, but a dagger-like pain seared through his leg. Josh lay back, dizzy and feeling sick as everything faded into black and white, then gray—then nothingness.

When Josh awoke again, he was in his own hospital room and, this time, it was his dad looking down at him. A wry smile crept across Josh's face. He didn't know whether to feel happy or scared. His father never seemed to have time to see him, so something very serious must be wrong.

"What's? What's going on? What happened?" Josh wondered why his words came slowly and slurred.

"They didn't tell you, Josh?" His dad's face looked warm and worried. It was good—so good just seeing his dad obviously concerned about him. But Josh could hardly contain his impatience.

"Tell me what? What happened?" Josh tried to move but his body wouldn't cooperate. It felt detached—heavy. "Why can't I move?"

"You don't remember the accident, son? Last night's freezing rain. The police didn't cite anybody because the pavement was so slick—no one's fault. You'll be OK, Josh. Thank God!"

Josh watched with wonder at the care lines etched on his father's face.

"Please, Josh, don't try to move," his dad went on. "You've got lots of bruises, a mild concussion, and a broken leg, but the doctors say you'll be as good as new in a few months. Sure scared us though, Josh!"

"Where's Mom?"

"Asleep on the bench in the corridor outside your door. She's been awake all night," his dad said.

"All night?" Josh exclaimed. "I thought you were in Chicago on business again. You're always gone! And Mom's been working night and day as usual. I never see either one of you, and when I do, you're too busy to talk." Josh's voice trailed off as he saw the effect of his words on his father who looked both grave and embarrassed at the same time.

"Your mom called me at midnight. I caught the first plane out. Got here an hour ago. Josh—I'm," and after a long pause, he added softly, "I'm sorry. Josh, one of the main reasons I'm working so hard is for your education, you know."

Josh looked out the window. It was snowing now and the sill was piled high with the cold white fluff. Were his father's words just so much cold white fluff? He wondered when he would be able to walk or run again, and how impossibly far behind he would get in all his classes. He thought of Jill who seemed to really care about him and enjoy his company, but why had she always refused him when he asked her out? And when would he ever see her again?

"Dad, it's good you're here. Thanks for that. But college—how can I ever hope to get in if I can't even handle the math? I don't know how I am going to manage with this broken leg." His voice choked as he blurted out, an octave higher, "I don't know how I'm going to manage a lot of things!"

"Son," his Dad said, softly, "I'll help you—don't worry." He pulled his chair close beside the bed and reached for Josh's trembling hand.

"Now tell me, son, what all is bothering you?"

Their eyes met and for the first time in years, Josh felt there was hope in their relationship.

"I hear voices!" Josh's mother said as she poked her head in at the doorway, then rushed over to plant an awkward kiss on Josh's forehead.

Josh grinned a crooked grin, then looked sullenly away. Did it take this to bring them together? Did he have to break his body to get their attention?

Just then there was a knock on the door and a chaplain asked permission to enter.

"May I be of any assistance?" he asked. "How are you feeling?" The kindly man looked straight at Josh.

"Broken," came Josh's quick reply.

"Yes, I see. Much pain?" The chaplain asked.

"Lots,—in lots of ways."

"I guess you're sharing some of the same pain of our Lord." The chaplain went on. "His body, too, was broken. He, too, felt pain in many ways."

Then, glancing around at Josh's mom and dad, he added. "But His brokenness brought people together. It drew them close—joining them in love."

Later that day, long after the chaplain and his parents had gone, the door opened to another surprise. It was Jill, bringing him some fresh water. She almost dropped the pitcher when she saw him.

"Josh!" she exclaimed. "What happened to you? I missed you at school, but had no idea!"

"Jill, you work here?!"

"Yes. Now you see why I could never accept your invitations! I work full-time here, 3:00 to 9:00, five days a week."

"Full-time! Why? How come, Jill?"

"Long story." Jill grinned. "But you?"

Josh just lay there smiling. Suddenly the tinseled garlands draping the hospital doorway looked cheery.

"Well," he murmured, "looks as if this will be a merry Christmas after all."

Somehow, Josh felt there was hope. Jill had problems perhaps he could share. His parents were there for him, now. Oh, his problems remained, all right—they were even larger, now. But he wasn't alone.

"Merry Christmas, Josh." Jill's eyes were tender.

# Eduardo's Homecoming

It was Christmas Eve, and Eduardo was not where he wanted to be. His heart ached to be with his mother and brothers and sisters in Mexico. His family circle was broken.

Eduardo was living with his father in a series of packing crate boxes on the edge of town. They were very, very poor. People called them "wetbacks" because they had come across the great Rio Grande River so they could find work and take money back for food and presents for Eduardo's mother and brothers and sisters. There were so many mouths to feed and so little money back at their home. But they had not yet earned enough to go back.

And now Eduardo's father was very sick. His face burned so hot, burning with the fever that came on during the day while he was working. His father thought, "If only I could lie down, I will be better."

But now it was night; he was lying down, and he was not better. Sometimes he was shivering cold and pulled Eduardo close to stop his shaking, but when Eduardo touched him, he felt very hot!

"Eduardo, I am so cold!" His father's body was wracked with chills.

"Caliente!" Eduardo protested that his father was hot, not cold.

Eduardo thought very hard, and a plan came to him. He covered his father's wracked body with his own jacket and the few newspapers he found near the trash barrel.

"I will get help for you," he said. "I will go for the padre. He will know what to do."

Eduardo hugged his shoulders with his bare, cold hands trying ever so hard to keep warm as he ran toward the great cathedral. His shirt felt as thin as the tissue paper of the festivals; icy wind glued it to his body.

The cathedral has many padres. "It is a great place, and surely somebody there can send good help for my father," Eduardo thought.

But as he came nearer, he could see that there was a service.

"Oh, yes! Of course!" He realized. "It is midnight Mass for it is Christmas Eve. But that means that all the padres will be busy."

The music of the service became louder as he neared, and the lights from the great stained glass windows looked warm and welcoming. He could see the many large cars and people crowding into the cathedral.

"It will be warmer inside," he thought, if I can only make it there. I am so tired and cold." He decided to take a shortcut through an alleyway.

Suddenly, Eduardo tripped and fell headlong, twisting his body badly. Pain pierced through his leg, and his breath came in frosted pants as he gripped his leg with his hands.

Eduardo knew that he could not stand on that leg. He also knew that he could not stand the cold very long and that his father was very, very sick and alone.

A wind began whipping down the forlorn passageway. Eduardo let out a shrill call for help, stifling it as soon as it was out. Fear gripped him as he realized that he was alone in that alleyway, and whatever kind of person might respond to his call? Eduardo painfully dragged his leg into the shadows and huddled against the cold.

He had to think, but he became dizzy. All that he seemed able to think of was his mother's smiling face as she clapped the tortillas between her hands, flattening them to fry in the skillet. He could almost hear her singing "Nito Lindo."

He thought of the warm fire under her skillet, and stretched out his fingers toward it in his mind. Now she was laughing happily, and he longed to be with her.

"I can't think of that or I'll die," he thought. "I must think of what to do! Maybe I can drag my leg to the end of the alley. Then I can get help when the Mass is over."

It hurt a lot to move. He tried very hard and managed to move a few feet at a time before he had to rest again from the pain.

The dizziness was on him once more, but this time he thought of his father. His poor father in such suffering—so sick. "If he should die—oh, no. I will not think of that. He works so hard. He tries so hard. He loves us all very much. Please, dear God, help him!"

Now Eduardo was moving—slowly inching his way down the dark corridor. He could hear the Kyrie now and the responses.

"I will. With God's help, I will! he said to himself.

He crossed himself and reached his hand out once again, only to feel a crushing blow to his arm. Terror struck him as he realized someone's large shoe had pinned his arm. As his eyes traveled upward through the darkness, he heard a rough voice demand, "Who are you?"

Eduardo tried to speak, but nausea squeezed his stomach, and the alley began to turn around him—all spilled into blackness.

The sickening blackness came and went as rough hands quickly went through his pockets. Finding nothing, a rough hand struck a blow to Eduardo's head before retreating down the alley.

The final hymn of the Mass was all that Eduardo could hear. It seemed to wrap around a vision of his parents together around the table with his brothers and sisters. They were all smiling happily and holding hands for the blessing.

People were leaving the cathedral now, and cars were starting. The sidewalks echoed with the sound of clicking heels and voices greeting each other with "Merry Christmas!"

"Oh! What's this?" a lady's voice said as she stopped short, noting a small hand reaching out from the dark alley.

She and her husband quickly knelt, and discovering poor Eduardo, covered him with their coats and solicitude. It wasn't long before he lay on a couch in the rectory with warm broth being poured gently between his white lips and a doctor sent for from the parish family. As soon as Eduardo could speak and his story told, the mercy of God and Christmas reigned on Eduardo. His father was fetched, and they were wrapped in warmth and healing love. They shared beds, Eduardo and his father, in the charity ward of the hospital until they were well enough to be sent back to their family in Mexico.

Now they have sponsors in the United States, and before many months, Eduardo's family encircled their own table in an apartment near the cathedral where Eduardo's father had a position as a caretaker.

When Eduardo next heard the Kyrie at Christmas midnight Mass, he knelt beside his father and mother in the great cathedral, and his eyes wandered smilingly down the pew to his brothers and sisters..

# The Yule Fire

The flames whip sideways, twisting and turning and licking the top of the fireplace. It is a fine fire this cold Christmas Eve as I lie on the soft rug and gaze at it, dreaming all sorts of imaginings.

Now I imagine a house afire and smoke billowing out from the windows as flames whip through the roof. I can hear the fire engines and see them coming.

Now I see firefighters scrambling all over the house. Each flame of the fireplace fire is a person who is working hard to put out the fierce blaze with hoses and nozzles and water sprays.

Now I see a lady who is leaning out of the top window with her face contorted with fear, and firefighters are trying to get the ladder close enough for her to reach.

Nope, can't do it. She'll have to jump, but she's too scared.

Now I see a little boy up there and he's holding something but I can't tell what. Oh! Now I see. It's his squirmy puppy and he's leaning out of the window, holding tightly to his puppy.

Now he's jumping out of the window, holding that little puppy close in his arms. The firefighters catch him with their little round net and he bounces right back up, and down, and up, and then the lady in the window looks at him and she smiles. The lady is not afraid anymore and, if the boy with the puppy ever stops bouncing, the lady can jump, too.

But the boy just keeps on jumping like he's on a trampoline, and the doggie's long ears go up and down—up when they're going down and down when they're going up.

But I don't think the lady's going to make it. She looks very angry and then scared again, and the firefighters are mad at the boy and yell at him to stop jumping. But he just grins and keeps on jumping.

Now the lady's too hot and she just jumps anyway, a little farther out. The firefighters are quick to notice, and they move the net ever so deftly and catch the lady. The little boy with the dog lands on his backside in the flower bed. The doggy runs away yelping, and the boy just sits there in a daze.

"Is everybody out?" the firefighter asks. Now the lady says "Yes," and swoons into the firefighter's arms while the fire is put out on her house.

So, that's over.

Well, now I think I see something beautiful in my fireplace fire. It is people and flowers and sugerplums and, how they dance!

The music swells and then it turns all dreamy and makes me sleepy. I close my eyes and now I'm dancing, too. I'm going around and around as I twirl through flowers and candy canes. I am getting very dizzy, but I keep on going around and around.

And around.

And around.

The fire is all gone as I open my eyes and what is this? I am so sleepy. I rub my eyes trying to see what this is because I hear something different. I see a soot-covered man with a round nose wearing a dirty white fur-collared suit, sticking his head out of the fireplace.

I close my eyes again. Of course, I am dreaming. I am so sleepy and I feel as if I am being lifted and wafted up the stairs to my bed. Someone plants a smooch on my forehead but I don't even open my eyes. Too sleepy.

"Merry Christmas, Sport!"

I bolt up, electric-like. There's Dad and Mom and the sun's up and I rub my eyes.

"Come on, sleepyhead!" Never thought you'd sleep in on Christmas morning!" Dad says.

Mom's smiling as we walk fast to the stairs.

"What's this on your forehead?" she asks. "Looks like a kiss mark, but it's not lipstick."

She runs her fingers across my forehead and holds out her hand for us all to see.

"Soot?!"

# The Legend of the Holly

There is a legend that the holly
wound 'round His head,
and great drops of crimson blood
against the green, they bled.

The holly mocked, as if a crown
of laurel for a king;
yet intertwined were cruel thorns
that pierced—a blood-let ring.

The sharp pain tore His tender brow,
but that was only part;—
for penetrating, O, so deep—
it broke His tender heart.

The Father said, "Forevermore
the holly tree shall bear
crimson berries with the green
like laid once in His hair.

And thorns would never form again
upon the holly tree,
but berries red, and prickly leaves
would be for all to see."

At Christmastide the wreaths are formed
of holly green and red—
reminder of what our dear Lord
had wound 'round His head.

# The Little Shepherd

Little God-Child, gentle One,
Awake in yonder manger,
You opened up your newborn eyes
and looked on me, a stranger!

How scared I was to see and hear
those angels full of joy!
They sang to me. (Yes—to me!)
A little shepherd boy.

First there was the one angel
who came within the night,
and told us not to be afraid—
then a great light shone so bright!

That angel said: "I bring to you
good tidings of great joy!"
Then told us how to go and find
this newborn baby boy.

*The angel said: "For unto you
is born this day . . . a savior. . . ."
Said we'd find You all wrapped up
and "lying in a manger."*

*Oh! Right away, the sky was filled
with thousands more, and then
they sang so mighty sweetly—
". . . on earth peace, good will to men."*

*So we came as fast as we could come
to Bethlehem—toward
where the angel said we'd find
our "Savior, Christ the Lord."*

*Oh little Baby thank you
for letting me come see
You who, they say, will be our hope
for all eternity.*

# The Crimson Christmas Ribbon

The red ribbon hung on the enamel-green bedpost. It drooped limply—a sagging reminder of the love of Christmas, of its hope and its joy.

A sardonic grimace crossed Grace's face as she looked from the crimson ribbon to the ash-white face of her three-year-old daughter as she lay against the stark-white hospital bed pillow.

Ironically, Grace had tied the ribbon jauntily among Debbie's soft black curls before they set off for a visit to the brightly-lit mall.

So many distractions, so much to see, and yet, in retrospect, so much need for care.

The carol singers with crimson ribbons tied around their necks sang from a tiered platform. Crimson poinsettias in green metallic wrap with red-bowed ribbons trimmed that fateful fountain—the fountain that fascinated Debbie, drawing her, mesmerizing her. That fountain that shot sprays of water sporadically higher to fall frothing and foaming into the green, marble-rimmed circle of a pond.

"Don't get too close!" Grace warned. She only looked away for a moment. And then she heard Debbie's scream. And then she heard nothing except the blood pounding in her ears.

Grace clawed them away—those masses of poinsettias circling the pool. And then she saw her floating in the water, and it was Debbie's own blood that swirled against the green marble pond among the frothing white waters of the fountain spray. It was as if her red ribbon was growing larger and broader. But it was not her ribbon, now.

It was not the Christmas ribbon that floated red from Debbie's forehead as her mother pulled her into anxious arms. They rose, dripping from the cold waters onto the spilled poinsettias into the dazed gathering crowd.

"Deb! Deb! Wake up!" Grace implored as she buried her ear into the soggy wetness of her daughter's blouse, listening for her heartbeat. She squeezed her face close to Debbie's hoping to feel her breath. But Debbie didn't open her eyes; she couldn't wake up.

The ambulance was quick. They frantically tried artificial respiration, wrapping her in blankets. As the siren blared through holiday traffic, and as Grace watched numbly, attendants applied thick gauze pads to Debbie's head—quickly reddening thick gauze pads. Absently, Grace picked up from the floor the limp wet ribbon that had fallen from Debbie's hair. Her hands squeezed it dry. Her heart churned in prayer. "Lord, let her be all right!"

Tom and Grace took turns at Debbie's side. During the first days, where her ribbon had been, white gauze wrapped her head. And where her smile was, a tube entered her nose and throat. Her eyes were forever shut and a needle sent nourishment into her hand.

Today, the doctor was going to talk with them there beside Debbie's bed. He wanted them together, he said, so they could share his information.

"I see no hope," he stated flatly. "We've done all we can. The tubes can supply her with nourishment; we can keep her body alive indefinitely." How were their monetary resources, he wanted to know, implying huge costs. He said they alone could decide whether she lived or died.

He spoke as if she were already gone, their Debbie. Their love. Their baby. Their child. Their hope and joy.

"But surely . . . ," they implored.

"I see no hope." And he turned on his heels and was gone down the antiseptic white corridor, disappearing with their hope, leaving only despair.

Grace started to run after him down the dead-white hall into oblivion. Cold and numb, she returned into Tom's trembling arms and together they wept—the tears a merciful hot salve.

Back in Debbie's room, Tom ran his fingers through her dark, curly hair—so soft and silky still.

Grace kissed her fingertips.

Grace looked again at the crimson Christmas ribbon and suddenly she knew that this she could fix. She could smooth out its sad, limp look and bend it again into a Christmas bow.

No longer able to utter words, her hands formed this prayer. It was an act of faith.

As her hands worked feverishly, the crimson Christmas ribbon yielded to furious efforts. She saw again the happy look of Christmas and all it stands for and reached for the bedpost to attach this small triumph of hope.

"Mom." Grace couldn't believe it. She couldn't breathe. But she turned and stared at her daughter. Tom, astonished, paused from stroking her hair.

"Mom. It goes in my hair," said Debbie.

Her voice choked on the tube and she coughed. She looked up at her dad who grinned incredulously. "It's my Christmas ribbon," and she smiled.

# The Petticoat of Heaven

Papa is gray, like the bleached-wood sides of the house where the sun long ago baked off the paint and the wind blew her own color on—a nothing color. Mama was sometimes gray, but when she smiled and when she laughed, she was the warm color of honey and daffodils like those she cherished down by the well.

And sometimes she was deep fuschia and rose like cactus flowers and sometimes sky-blue, but when she died she was white and papa grew grayer and grayer like the boulders of the canyon and the bent-over mesquite trees and the tumbleweed blowing in the dust-wind.

But Papa is not like tumbleweed; Papa works all the time from before the sun comes up and while it blisters and blusters across the big sky until it dies in the west. And now that Mama's gone, it's like the days are all gray, too, and my life is gray and I look out of my gray window that is in the loft where I can see maybe a hundred miles. My window has gray screen that is patched with gray wire and I put my chin in my hand and try to see another color.

When Mama was sick, she'd lay on the iron bed here by the window and I would fan her with castor bean leaves to keep the mosquitoes away. And she would look out and marvel at the blueness of the sky and make all kinds of imaginings about the clouds, saying, "Look here—a lamb, and it's sailing along as if it has wings," or "Look at that big cloud! It's grinning at you!" or "There's a lovely lady in a long white wedding dress—so elegant and fine—all satin and lace."

And when the sun would lower to the west, there would be grand patterns of sweet-fine colors. Mama would say that that was the "petticoat of Heaven showing," and she'd tell me how much more beautiful it was further up where we couldn't see, and that we would go there one day. And she went, but she left me here! Now my nothing-colored tears taste like the sand of the desert and I cry loudly, "Mama! Show me the petticoat of Heaven again!"

That was in the spring when we watched the heavens together. We could open the window curtains all day but when summer came it was too hot and we had to close the curtains to keep out the heat after breakfast until near supper-time.

And in the summer the sun clawed its way over the forever-sky, searing it and us and anything else in its path. It was a giant-burning-coneflower that never dried up. But it left everything the color of ashes when it was gone.

Sometimes, the sun dimmed to a dull brick red with an orange halo and it got dark and I prayed it would rain, and I heard sounds like sleet on the windows, but mama said it was only sand blowing in the fierce wind. No matter how tightly we closed the doors and windows, stuffing rags along the edges, when the wind blew down and the darkness lightened, there was always a layer of sand on everything in the house and we dusted and swept for hours to clean up after the sandstorms of last summer.

But then summer passed and Mama with it and what had been warm turned cold and northers blew in heat lightning and thunder but still no rain eased the drought. The sky always looked angry and Mama's fluffy clouds were all blown away and with them all my world of warmth and color.

Now, as I look clear across the bare flat land to the edge

of the horizon where the charcoal-dead sky meets the dry-bare land, I think I see something slowly moving. Not the tumbleweed that blows swirly around—it is moving straight and it is moving ever so slowly this way across the mesa from down by the Rio. It looks like a couple of tiny ants. It is moving toward me very slowly and I wonder and I strain to see and I wait, fascinated that something new is coming into my life.

Now I think it is maybe a person or two people or a person and a horse and then I see better when the wind swirls the dust away for a short split second, and I think that it looks like maybe a man and a donkey that he is walking, and I hold my breath because of the excitement because we don't have many visitors and I am thinking—what can I give them? I think of the few peaches Mama and I canned and I am thinking of biscuits, but there is hardly any flour left and the year is dying like Mama was and there's not much of anything left in our root cellar either in this time of the dying of the year after the bandidos came and took what they did. And someone is coming. I can slice the mush left from breakfast and fry it in lard, I am thinking; there's still cornmeal and there's still lard.

And then I see the wind pile up white clouds in with the gray as it howls and I see the person bent into the wind and walking hard to move against the cold north gusts. He is still like a small speck very far to the south and will be a long time getting to our house.

So I smooth the bed cover and climb down the ladder and sweep hard at the dust and the sand all the time thinking of how Mama and I cleaned last winter about this time of year for Christmas, but there won't be any Christmas this year. Papa doesn't believe. And he's tired and he hasn't money, but mostly Mama's gone and with her the presents she made with her hands when we weren't around to see. The new shirts for Papa and the dress for me and my rag doll with the saffron yellow-gold hair plaited so smoothly into pigtails, and—best of all—the corn-husk crèche.

She wrapped these in funny-papers and strung dried berries and paper chains on mesquite branches, tying a gold foil star to the top.

Now my stomach churns and my chest aches and I whisper "Mama, Mama," and run up the ladder for another look.

And now I freeze and all my feelings in my body turn cold and hot at what I am seeing. Papa, the color of thunder, with his long shotgun, and him standing with his two legs far apart like they were planted in the clay-dust—staring down the rutted road.

And now I see and understand. He's looking at who's coming. The man is bent into the wind so far his sombrero top is almost all we can see, but he's pulling hard on a donkey burdened with a piled up load wrapped in the most beautiful many-colored blanket I've ever seen. The colors dance even in the somber dusk like they're alive and the corners of my mouth go up and down not knowing what to feel. And then I look again at Papa and the wind is whipping at his shirt and hair and pant legs like flags in the breeze and he stands gaunt and lifts his shotgun.

As I slide down the ladder, splinters tearing into my legs and hands, I know that Papa's remembering the bandidos who rode up that same rutted road. He's remembering them and what they did to us, but he's forgetting the poor families hungry for food, who swim the Rio Grande looking for work to feed the ones they love.

"Papa! Bandidos don't pull donkeys! They ride horses! Papa

don't!" But I was too late. The stranger turned off the road at the crack of Papa's gun and headed into the canyon where tarantulas dance with rattlers and only coyotes dare enter.

And now I'm running, barefoot through boulders by the arroyo. Snakes hide in the crevices all winter long here, blind and quick to strike, their skins shed like silver camisoles in the sun-dried paths I follow.

And now, finally, the rain that wouldn't come in the searing summer falls slant and hard—sleek, shiny silver-bullet-rain pelting my body like ice, wetting my thin cotton dress, making my chin chatter and freezing my choked-up anguish.

Now I see them—the man with the donkey and he looks at me with fear in his eyes but I see beyond them into the pain and he jumps beside the blanket on the donkey, with his back to it and his front to me and his arms trying to bend backward to protect and hold it.

And I say, "Don't worry! I want to help you!" but he just shakes his head like he doesn't understand.

And now I hear a little cry like a baby and his arms turn him around to encircle the many-colored blanket and it moves and yields to his embrace and I see that it is a woman and a very tiny baby in that blanket. The mother's eyes look at me and back to her baby and once again I see the warm color of honey and daffodils under the blanket and I also see the color of deep fuschia and rose, like cactus flowers mixed with cornflower-blue.

They are following me, and my head is sheltered from the rain by his many-colored serape. He is sheltering his family with the many-colored blanket as he walks beside the donkey.

In the barn, now, I push the old gray hay aside, furiously scooping up the sweet, yellow honey-colored hay that lays below the surface. With this I make a bed for the baby. Now I worry about Papa and motion to these three to stay, and I go out in the cold to find Papa.

And I find him curled down in his rocker with his head in his hands bent over almost to his torn and mud-coated boots. He is crying and I have never seen him cry. And it's Mama gone and it's remembering the bandits, and it's the farm—burnt and bare from the drought—and it's me gone and him not believing and not knowing if he hurt somebody with his shotgun—everything at once—and I put my arms around him and he can't stop sobbing like in a convulsion of all the tears from a great-long-pain so I pet him and wrap my arms around his shaking wet shoulders and smell the rain mixed with Papa smells of sweat and work and salt-tears.

After awhile our sobbing stops and now I am frying corn mush in the hot lard and the smell is good and Papa is spicing the elderberry tea with cloves Mama saved for Christmas. When we get it all fixed and bundled and start out across to the barn with Papa's lantern, we see candles burning in paper sacks by the barn doors.

And there they are—the baby in the middle with him and her on each side just like in Mama's corn-husk creche.

"Feliz Navidad!" they say.

And in their faces, the candle flickers all amber like honey and daffodils. And the many-colored blanket sends its colors flickering through candle-flames and I think of heaven's many colored petticoats.

# Stranded in a Snowstorm

They walked in through the door one by one, clapping the snow off their coats and chilled hands, tramping it off their boots and shoes. Some blew frosted breath into blue-veined hands, cupping them over their faces to feel the scant warmth. They made little dancing motions, slapping their sides. All save three—the old man with the contorted body who stood in silent acquiescence to his cold and pain; also the young woman and the bundle she so carefully sheltered with her arched body.

The last one in turned to look behind him into the storm, squinting to see if anyone followed. Satisfied that he was, indeed, the last, he heaved the heavy door shut and sank, exhausted, to the earth floor with his weight against the door. as if trying in some way to extinguish the storm.

Slowly, their eyes became accustomed to the darkness and each, in his or her own way appraised the situation.

"What the—?" We shoulda' stayed in the bus!" It was the burly one with the blonde. She looked at him sullenly.

"We woulda' frozen ifn we'd stayed," came the driver.

"It's a miner's cabin," came the young soldier. " See his pans in the corner? But is that all the wood for the fireplace—two logs."

"If we'd stayed, the troopers woulda' come cleanin' the road 'n found us. Think they'll ever find us here?" the burly one again.

The young woman with the bundle lifted the torn sheet partition and looked at the empty coverless bunk. The others peered through, then back at the main section of the cabin.

There were a few cracked dishes, some mugs and a tin of sardines on the table in one corner.

A stool and kettle rested by the hearth. The soldier opened the cabinet and found two tins of beans, a bucket and a fork and spoon. A long bench, mismatched chairs, dust and cobwebs remained to decorate the room.

While the others examined the place, the contorted old man knelt in front of the fireplace and with seeming experience, soon had a small fire started.

The young woman smiled shyly and sat on the stool beside him with her bundle, opening a small peek-hole to the sleeping child. Assured, she quickly closed it again and started swaying to and fro.

"That wood won't last," the soldier arched his brows. "Someone has to go out."

Silently, eyes sought one another. A few sighs punctuated the silence.

The blonde fixed her eyes on the burly one. "You promised we'd be back before Christmas! Now look! If they catch us here together—well, you know."

"You think I planned this?" he came back angrily.

The old man rose, his hands painfully raised like a benediction. The others noticed, turning their attention to the half-smile on his face.

"It's Christmas eve." He measured the words, looking almost like a pastor blessing his flock.

There were a couple of quick breaths in the silence that followed, as if rejoinders were about to be made but stifled. For a moment, warmth replaced the strained fear in the young mother's eyes. The blonde looked at the ceiling, her thumbs nervously twitching, then she caught the sardonic gaze of her companion. The soldier looked wistfully at the fire. The driver gave a half-laugh and turned to peer out of the soiled window-pane toward the abandoned bus that lay below the snow-swept hill. Occasionally, a lull in the whirling snow allowed him to see the clipped cadence of its emergency lights.

For a time all were lost in their own reveries. The baby's cry startled them back to the present. The mother quickened her rocking motions and hummed a soft lullaby, but the baby's needs would not be so easily satisfied. The young mother looked contemplatively toward the curtain and rose, excusing herself behind its thin protection.

The blonde got up and stood by the curtain.

"All right, fellas," she stated. "Feeding time. Let's give mama some privacy."

"Hey, where'd the old man go?" It was the burly one who first noticed the absence.

"What the . . . ?" Eyes shot through the dim corners and back. The soiled window shade was pushed back while incredulous faces sought signs of the missing companion. Through the blur of swirling snow, his bent and labored form took shape, bearing toward the cabin. The soldier threw the door open and ran to meet him, lifting the sticks of wood from his shoulder and taking the bucket from his cold gnarled hand—pushed him toward the gaping door.

They laid him on the bench. The driver removed his slicker and laid it over the old man's shaking body. The blonde massaged his cold hands while the soldier stacked the wood by the fire to dry.

"What's in the bucket? Snow! Is that just lousy snow?" the burly one asked.

'To drink, you fool!" the soldier muttered as he placed some in the kettle and set it to boil, carefully resting it on the swinging iron hook over the fire. "Hot water's at least warmin'."

He turned to face the group.

"O.K., you guys, we've got to get organized. We don't need any more repeats of what just happened."

All looked at the old man who lay silently on the bench, breathing slowly and with effort. As if on impulse, the burly one removed his jacket, folded it once as he crossed the cabin to the bench, knelt and carefully slipped it under the old man's head and shoulders. For a moment their eyes met and the old man forced a labored smile; the burly one twisted in embarrassment.

As the young mother emerged from behind the curtain with her contented child the driver hastily rose to offer her his chair.

"It's warmer now," she exclaimed. "Oh, thank you!"

"What's the kid? A boy or a girl?" the blonde asked.

"A boy." And she opened the bundle to let them all see.

Smiles warmed the faces even as the fire warmed the room.

"Like I said," the soldier tried again. "We've got to get organized. We might be here a long while." He caught the quick look of fear on the mother's face. "If we're careful, we can make it. But we gotta be careful!"

"Yeah," said the burly one skeptically. "What's your ideas?"

"The soldier's right," the driver said. "Listen to him."

"O.K. My plan? We've got to keep plenty of water and keep warm. That means foraging trips—two by two. No more singles." All eyes went to the old man.

"Wait a minute." The soldier lined up ill assorted mugs on the hearth. With a poker and his scarf, he managed to pour scalding water from the kettle over the cups to clean them; then he filled them half full with hot water and passed them around. They all savored the warmth in their hands and sipping the hot fluid, felt the chill ease from their bodies.

More receptive now, they looked back to the soldier who raised his hand for attention.

"The water's not hard to get—melted snow." he said. "We just gotta keep the kettle 'n bucket full at all times. But we'll take turns getting wood."

The old man was sitting up now, the warm cup rotating in his arthritic hands. He spoke, his voice soft, but they all strained to listen.

"There's a small lean-to horse-stall 'bout five yards to the south with an outhouse beside it. There's hay in the stall, and wood stacked beside."

"Great!" came the soldier. There were smiles all around.

"But food! You fools—what's good about water and no food!" the burly one broke in.

The soldier stood up. "Just keep your belly full of water for now. Help'll come."

So two by two, the occupants of the miner's cabin ventured into the storm; the women returned with hay and the men with wood.

Hours later, the snow plow made its way toward the bus which sat cockeyed in the ditch with emergency lights still clicking. The patrol car following the plow stopped and two weary officers scratched their heads.

"Empty."

"Where could they have gone?"

"Maybe another vehicle picked them up."

"What vehicle?!"

"Hey—look up on that hill. Maybe that cabin with the smoke."

As the officers approached the cabin, strains of carols reached their ears and sounds of merry-making.

As the door opened to their knock, they stepped inside to see a babe lying in the straw of what looked to be a manger with its radiantly smiling mother along side. The pungent smell of baked beans came from the cheery hearth, while someone thrust warm mugs into their hands.

"Uh,—I'm sorry to interrupt your party," the officer smiled. "Just looking for some stranded travelers caught in the storm. Have you seen or heard of any up this way?"

# Out of Egypt I Called My Son

*"Out of Egypt I called my Son. . . ."*
Hosea 11:1 and Matthew 2:15

In Egypt there are wonderful stories of the Holy Family little known elsewhere in the world. These have been told from father and mother to child for hundreds of years. They tell of the path the Holy Family took in these fabled Egyptian lands and also of wonderful happenings that surrounded that flight. These stories are treasured by Christian and Muslim alike in Egypt, although they vary a little at times. But whether fact or fiction, in whole or in part (as they may have been embroidered or embellished many times), one thing is certain: They are held close to the hearts of a people fervent with a love of God.

*"Arise, and take the Child and his mother, and flee into Egypt, and remain there until I tell thee. For Herod will seek the Child to destroy him"* (Matthew 13), the angel told Joseph in a dream. It fulfilled a prediction made centuries earlier when the prophet Hosea said, *"Out of Egypt I called my son"* (Hosea 11:1).

It is believed the Holy Family followed a path close by the sea across the Sinai, entering a village called Ismailia in Egypt. From there they continued on to Tal Basta near the present town of Zagazig close to the eastern edge of the Nile River delta.

At Tal Basta, stories tell of a man named Aqloum who took pity on the Holy Family, inviting them to his home for food and rest. Aqloum's wife, a bedridden invalid, was said to have been healed during the visit. Also at Tal Basta, a story tells of a well from which the Holy Family drank and how the waters from that well became known for their healing powers. At another town, Joseph asked for bread for the Christ-Child and it was refused. To this day, Egyptians insist that bread will not rise in the village where this occurred!

Just south of Tal Basta, in the town of Bilbeis, another story tells of a mother who wept for her dying son, Jacob, and how, as the Holy Family passed, the son arose and was well.

From here the Holy Family turned northward toward a town called Meniet Samannoud and, again, the family grew thirsty but there was no water to be found. The stories vary about this, but somehow water flowed from a stone and became a treasured well. The tiny footprint of the Christ-Child remained on this stone and the place is known as Picha Isos meaning, "the heel of Jesus."

From here the Holy Family is said to have crossed the Nile and moved deep within the hot deserts of western Egypt, for word of the Holy Family's sojourn in Egypt had passed back to Herod and it was not prudent to stay long in any one place. However, they spent some time in the deep desert valley known as Wadi el Natrun which became, in later centuries, the site of many monasteries continuing to this day.

Out of these deserts they moved eastward across the Nile toward the ancient city of Babylon (Cairo) and rested under a tree in the city of Heliopolis. This is the ancient seat of learning where Moses was educated.

This place is preserved today and known as the Virgin Tree, and one can go there and view a most ancient-looking gnarled tree beside a very old well. It is surrounded by a high protective wall, separating it from the teaming city of Cairo that has grown to surround Heliopolis. But it is like a quiet oasis, this Virgin Tree place, tended by gentle people who seem to have moved back in time to the days of the holy sojourn. And there is a quiet here and a peace and serenity that belies understanding. The story goes that Mary washed the clothes of the Christ-Child in the well and that wherever a drop of water fell, a balsam tree grew. There is a history of a grand grove of these tall trees growing on the desert sands, but they have all vanished and the tree and well are all that remain today.

From here the Holy Family is believed to have traveled into Babylon, known today as Old Cairo—an enclave of ancient churches and a synagogue within the heart of modern Cairo. It is told that the Holy Family lived here in a cave for several months. Saint Sergius church stands above this cave and from inside one can peer down a flight of steps to where the waters of the Nile bathe those ancient stones which once held the Christ-Child, Mary and Joseph.

From Babylon, the Family moved south toward the Nile and as they neared a temple that stood on the banks of the river, an earthquake shook the area, toppling the idols within. The prophet Isaiah, had said, "Oracle on Egypt: See, the Lord is riding on a swift cloud on his way to Egypt; the idols of Egypt tremble before him, the hearts of the Egyptians melt within them" (Isaiah 19:1). As the family approached, the earth became calm and they were able to sleep within its walls and refresh themselves before setting sail on a boat against the tide up the River Nile.

This happened at a town called Maadi, and every year the father of the church there embarks on a boat, as the Holy Family once did in commemoration of that event. People come from miles around and fill the Nile with their feluccas, celebrating with joy and singing the time of the presence of the Holy Family in their midst.

In their journey upstream on the Nile, at a narrow place beside a high mountain, Mary noticed a boulder poised as if to fall on their frail boat. It is told that the child Jesus extended his hand to hold back the stone, and that his palm print remained for all to see. This happened in Middle Egypt near Samalut at Gebel al Tair (Mount of the Birds).

Stories vary as to whether the Holy Family continued on a boat or by land, but most agree that they spent some time at a place near El Qusiya called Quasqam. There is a small stone there said to have been used as a pillow for the Christ-Child.

Wonderful cliffs with magnificent views stand near the Nile in Middle Egypt. It is believed that it was in a cave on one of these cliffs near the village of Durunka, south of Asyut that the angel again visited Joseph in a dream. "Arise, and take the child and his mother, and go into the land of Israel, for those who sought the child's life are dead" (Matthew 2:20).

Most believe the Holy Family returned as they came, but it is not always agreed as to which event happened in which direction! Neither is the length of the Egyptian stay agreed upon. Muslims generally hold to six years, while the Christians usually say it was three and a half years. The Koran mentions how the date palm tree sustained the Holy Family, giving nourishment as well as shelter. In the Franciscan church on top of Mt. Nebo in Jordan, there is the date tree motif in reference to the Holy Family's survival in alien lands. No one knows the truth of these stories which may or may not have been embroidered many times; but the essence is there that once a marvelous Family did, indeed, visit Egypt.

There is another story told of how two thieves robbed the Holy Family during their Egyptian sojourn, and how one of them eventually was crucified on a cross beside Jesus. It was he who repented and to whom Jesus said, "Amen, I say unto thee, this day thou shalt be with me in Paradise" (Luke 23:43).

# Listen! Christmas Angels

From the beginning of time, angels brought wonderful and marvelous news to those who would listen. When Jesus was born into the world—the very first Christmas—angels were very active in bearing glad tidings, advising and warning those they would protect. These angels were feared, doubted, questioned, and often left in awe and wonder those to whom they spoke. In the stories of their speakings, the entire Christmas story is told. Often, their key word was, "Listen!"

Luke tells us of the angels appearing to Zechariah, father-to-be of John the Baptist, forerunner of our Lord. Zechariah and his wife Elizabeth were getting on in years, childless, devout servers of the Lord. Zechariah was a priest in the temple. "Then an angel of the Lord appeared to him, standing at the right side of the altar of incense. When Zechariah saw him, he was startled and gripped with fear. But the angel said to him: 'Do not be afraid, Zechariah; your prayer has been heard. Your wife Elizabeth shall bear you a son, and you are to give him the name John. He will be a joy and a delight to you, and many will rejoice because of his birth, for he will be great in the sight of the Lord. He is never to take wine or other fermented drink, and he will be filled with the Holy Spirit, even from birth. Many of the people of Israel will he bring back to the Lord their God. And he will go on before the Lord, in the spirit and power of Elijah, to turn the hearts of the fathers to their children and the disobedient to the wisdom of the righteous—to make ready a people prepared for the Lord.' Zechariah asked the angel, 'How can I be sure of this? I am an old man and my wife is well along in years.' The angel answered, 'I am Gabriel. I stand in the presence of God, and I have been sent to speak to you and tell you this good news. And now you will be silent and not able to speak until this happens, because you did not believe my words, which will come true at their proper time'" (Luke 1:11–20).

Luke goes on to tell that in the sixth month, Gabriel appears to Mary. "In the sixth month, God sent the angel Gabriel to Nazareth, a town in Galilee, to a virgin pledged to be married to a man named Joseph, a descendant of David. The virgin's name was Mary. The angel went to her and said, 'Greetings, you who are highly favored! The Lord is with you.'

Mary was greatly troubled at his words and wondered what kind of greeting this might be. But the angel said to her, 'Do not be afraid, Mary, for you have found favor with God. You will be with child and give birth to a son, and you are to give him the name Jesus. He will be great and will be called the Son of the Most High. The Lord God will give him the throne of his father David, and he will reign over the house of Jacob forever; his kingdom will never end.'

'How shall this be,' Mary asked the angel, 'since I am a virgin'?

The angel answered, 'The Holy Spirit will come over you, and the power of the Most High will overshadow you. So the holy one to be born will be called the Son of God. Even Elizabeth, your relative, is going to have a child in her old age, and she who was said to be barren is in her sixth month. For nothing is impossible to God.'

'I am the Lord's servant,' Mary answered. 'May it be to me as you have said.' Then the angel left her" (Luke 1:26–38).

Not long after this appearance, Gabriel spoke to Joseph in a dream, as Matthew tells us. "This is how the birth of Jesus Christ came about: His mother Mary was pledged to be married to Joseph, but before they came together, she was found to be with child through the Holy Spirit. Because Joseph her husband was a righteous man and did not want to expose her to public disgrace, he had in mind to divorce her quietly. But after he had considered this, an angel of the Lord appeared to him in a dream and said, 'Joseph son of David, do not be afraid to take Mary home as your wife, because what is conceived in her is from the Holy Spirit. She will give birth to a son, and you will give him the name Jesus, because he will save his people from their sins.' All this took place to fulfill what the Lord had said through the prophet: 'The virgin will be with child and will give birth to a son, and they will call him Immanuel'—which means, 'God with us.' When Joseph woke up, he did what the angel of the Lord had commanded him and took Mary home as his wife. But he had no union with her until she gave birth to a son. And he gave him the name Jesus" (Matthew 1:18–25).

A few months later, the angels spoke again; this time it was to the shepherds. Luke tells this story: "And there were shepherds living out in the fields nearby, keeping watch over their flocks at night. An angel of the Lord appeared to them, and the glory of the Lord shone around them, and they were terrified. But the angel said to them, 'Do not be afraid. I bring you good news of great joy that will be for all the people. Today in the town of David a Savior has been born to you; he is Christ the Lord. This will be a sign to you: You will find a baby wrapped in cloths and lying in a manger.' Suddenly, a great company of the heavenly host appeared with the angel, praising God and saying,

Glory to God in the highest,
and on earth peace. . . . (Luke 2:8–14).

Like Joseph, the Wise Men, too, received news of great importance through a dream as told, here, by Matthew. "Then Herod called the Magi secretly and found out from them the exact time the star had appeared. He sent them to Bethlehem and said, 'Go and make a careful search for the child. As soon as you find him, report to me, so that I too may go and worship him.' After they had heard the king, they went on their way, and the star they had seen in the east went ahead of them until it stopped over the place where the child was. When they saw the star, they were overjoyed. On coming to the house, they saw the child with his mother Mary, and they bowed down and worshiped him. Then they opened their treasures and presented him gifts of gold and of incense and of myrrh. And having been warned in a dream not to go back to Herod, they returned to their country by another route" (Matthew 2:7–12).

And again the angels warned Joseph of danger, Matthew tells us. "When they had gone, an angel of the Lord appeared to Joseph in a dream. 'Get up,' he said, 'take the child and his mother and escape to Egypt. Stay there until I tell you, for Herod is going to search for the child to kill him.' So he got up, took the child and his mother during the night and left for Egypt, where he stayed until the death of Herod. And so fulfilled what the Lord had said through the prophet: 'Out of Egypt I called my son'" (Matthew 2:13–15).

And a little later, "After Herod died, an angel of the Lord appeared in a dream to Joseph in Egypt and said, 'Get up, take the child and his mother and go to the land of Israel, for those who were trying to take the child's life are dead.' So he got up, took the child and his mother and went to the land of Israel. But when he heard that Archelaus was reigning in Judea in place of his father Herod, he was afraid to go there. Having been warned in a dream, he withdrew to the district of Galilee, and he went and lived in a town called Nazareth. So was fulfilled what was said through the prophets: 'He was called a Nazarene'" (Matthew 2:19–23).

I wonder how many times we have been warned or advised or greeted in some way by angels, but have been unaware. And it is interesting to note that in these stories of Christmas angels, as well as in other famous stories of angels throughout history, their key word has often been, "Listen!"

# A Birthday Party for Jesus

It was early December. Elizabeth, Josh and Sam were thinking about Christmas. They all agreed that they would like some changes made in how they celebrated this grand event, but what these changes should be eluded them. It wasn't a matter of money, for the family was quite well off. In fact, their parents were very generous when it came to Christmas, realizing their blessings and attributing them all to the great, good Lord.

A most magnificent tree embellished with the loveliest of decorations filled the great hall each year. Now that Sam, the youngest child, no longer believed in Father Christmas, the day's events unrolled this way: generous, carefully chosen gifts lay gift wrapped beneath the tree. After services on Christmas Day, the family, with glowing faces, exchanged the presents, then sat down to a feast prepared by Ms. Mullins and the kitchen staff. Father always gave out ample Christmas checks to each employee and dropped a particularly large one in the Christmas offering at Church.

"Well," mused the eldest, Elizabeth, "It is a birthday. How about a birthday party for Jesus?"

"How?" Sam, who dearly loved parties, demanded to know, with a broad smile. "How could we do that?"

"It already is a birthday," came Josh, brightening a bit, "but not celebrated like one exactly." His words trailed off somewhat wistfully, his blue eyes narrowing over a scattering of freckles.

"For starters, we could have a cake—a birthday cake," Elizabeth advised her younger brothers, with tentative enthusiasm.

"Sure!" smiled Sam who liked birthday cakes over any other food. "With candles and decorations and all, but not red and green!"

"No. Not red and green!" Elizabeth agreed. "How about white cake with blue and yellow trim? White for pure, sweet Jesus and blue for heaven and yellow for the sunshine and happiness he brings?"

They all grinned, so that much was decided.

"And a party. A birthday party!" Sam, who dearly loved birthday parties fairly jumped for joy at the idea.

"But who would we invite?" Josh wondered, frowning a little. "Everyone wants to be home with their families on Christmas Day."

There was a long, thoughtful pause.

"There could be us, and Father and Mother of course," said Elizabeth. "And . . . uhh . . . how about inviting all the help?" She smiled expectantly, looking at each of her brothers who stared blankly back.

"I think the help would rather have the day off to be with their own families, don't you think?" came Josh, the thoughtful one.

Suddenly Elizabeth brightened. "Let's us be the 'help' and give the party and have what we always have for birthdays—lots of birthday cake and ice cream served with fruit punch filled with sliced limes and strawberries! We could even ask Ms. Mullins to prepare a great goose and plum pudding for us the day before, and we could heat them up in the oven or microwave for our party!"

"And our guests?" asked Josh again.

Another awkward silence.

Then Josh continued, slowly, "Uh, I remember a Bible story about inviting strangers along the highways and byways to a wedding feast. But how could we invite strangers who wouldn't be having their own nice Christmas to our party?"

"Ask Mum," said Sam.

"No, let's try to figure it out ourselves and surprise Mum and Father, too," said Elizabeth. "Sort of like a present for them, too."

"Then let's ask Pastor John," came Josh, and it was decided.

Elizabeth called for an appointment, and they all sloshed down to the rectory together, tramping in their galoshes through the wet snow, their frozen breath blowing in the wind.

"Well, well," smiled Pastor John. "What brings you three here today?" Whereupon they all started in at once. After some confusion, Elizabeth became the spokesperson and soon the plan was out, laid squarely at the feet of the pastor.

"My, my," murmured Pastor John, puffing on his pipe.

"And how many candles will you have on your cake?"

"Well," came Elizabeth. "I thought of buying a package of candles and spelling out 2000. Is that close enough, do you think?"

Pastor John nodded with a smile of admiration and approval. "But your guests, may I think about that for a while? How many did you have in mind?"

"It's not so much a matter of how many, Pastor John," Josh answered quickly, "but who would Jesus want to have at his party?"

Three pairs of earnest eyes stared eagerly into those of the intrigued Pastor, who rubbed his chin thoughtfully. He dodged their question with another.

"What do you have in mind for entertainment?"

The three children looked at each other. Josh cocked his head and raised his shoulders as if to say he had no idea. Sam was about to say "Games!" when Elizabeth interjected:

"That would depend on who we had for guests. What would please some might not please others."

"Had you thought," mused the Pastor, "that perhaps the most fun for everyone would be taking gifts—like toys to poor children, or food to the hungry, or clothes to the destitute just might be the most fun thing to do at Jesus' birthday party?"

There was just a moment of excited silence, then smiles wreathed the children's faces as they each exclaimed their joyous approval.

"Also, it might just really be fun to visit—really sit down and visit—with some old folks at the home, some sick folks at the hospital, and even someone in prison."

The children's eyes fairly danced with delight.

"About giving food and toys and clothes, I think I remember Jesus telling us to do such things in secret," the ever thoughtful Josh commented.

"Very good!" said the beaming Pastor. "Ahh, what about my giving you some names and addresses and needs, and you dropping off the things on their doorsteps, ringing the doorbells, then running away as fast as you can. I would be delighted to drive the church van and park it, say, a half square away from each stop so it could be done somewhat secretly."

"Do you think I am tall enough to dress up like Father Christmas?" Josh asked. At this, everyone laughed, but, in fact, Josh just might pass for Father Christmas, as he was, indeed, quite tall for his age.

With shining faces all around, they parted, agreeing to a second meeting in a few days to work further on their plans. They had accomplished much, but there was much left to do in working out the details. Besides, Pastor John needed time to think about names, needs and addresses.

In the meantime, the children began pooling their allowances and asked their parents discreetly for ways to earn more Christmas money, and the parents indulgently and happily found ways to fatten their children's accounts.

Elizabeth thought of making wreaths to go with the other presents and asked the gardener for trimmings from the holly and the ivy. Josh bent wire coat hangers into circles to which Sam and Elizabeth tied the evergreens. They bought a spool of red ribbon and soon the back of the old carriage house was stacked with fresh wreaths hidden under an old tarpaulin.

Sam solemnly announced that he had outgrown "all those baby toys" he pointed to at the back of the nursery. Some had even belonged to Elizabeth and Josh years before. Many were hardly used—like new. So these, too, were secreted away, carefully gift wrapped, and each marked "boy" or "girl" with an appropriate age.

Elizabeth asked permission to try her hand at some Christmas baking, so the children got control of the kitchen for several hours each week, gathered mincemeat recipes, and soon wonderful aromas wafted through the great house. Some were shared with their unsuspecting parents while others were tucked away in a corner of the freezer. Cook was sworn to secrecy!

So by the time of the second meeting with Pastor John, the project was well on its way.

"Come in! Come in!" It was hard to tell who was the most excited, the children or the pastor.

While the children told him all they'd been up to in preparation, the Pastor listened intently, marveling at this blessing in his life.

Then it was his turn, and he began slowly, tentatively.

"I've been thinking about your guest list and want you to tell me truthfully what you think. First off, I'd suggest you invite your parents. They certainly need to know as it is their house; you are their children; and they need to know in order to give their house help the day off. Then your parents could give them their Christmas checks and send them home to spend the holidays with their own families."

The children nodded eagerly.

"And I've inquired at the Children's Home and there are exactly ten children there who are your ages. Would you like to invite them?"

"A great idea!" Sam exclaimed.

"Then I thought of a few adults in town who are very lonely. Two are widows who live alone and have no family nearby—Widow Jones and Widow Bowers. Then there is old Jasper Higgins who lives on top of the hill who hasn't set foot in church since his wife died twenty years ago. He lives alone and is a bit of a scrooge, but I think this would be very good for him if he would come. That makes fifteen guests, including your parents plus me—I would love to come!—and the three of you. Nineteen people in all. Please be very honest. Do you want all of these people?"

"Yes!" the children cried in unison, eyes dancing. Sam actually danced a sort of jig while Elizabeth and Josh grinned at each other.

"And I've prepared another list," the pastor told them, "of stops on our delivery route, noting what might be most appreciated at each place—food, clothing (with sizes) and toys where appropriate. By the way, the widows sew," and the pastor winked.

Back home, Elizabeth devised an invitation; Josh cut and lettered them, and Sam painted each, individually, with his water colors. On each square sheet, Baby Jesus lay in his manger in the lower left corner. A star shone in the upper right corner, with rays streaming across the page to the Child, forming lines for the words which read:

You are invited to a birthday party!
Time: December 25 at 2:00 PM
Where: Our house (#7 Park Place)
To Honor: Baby Jesus (by doing what he said)
RSVP: Elizabeth, Josh & Sam #747-9800

Their parents received their invitations after dinner by the fire and gave their hearty approval. Mum was all a-dither about preparations but was told in no uncertain terms that she was a guest and was to do nothing but enjoy herself. Father slipped Elizabeth a large bill, winked, and got back to reading his paper.

The widow ladies were the first to call, wanting to know how they planned to honor Baby Jesus, and when they were told, they insisted on bringing some food and doing some sewing. So Elizabeth gave each some names and sizes for children's clothing. All but three of the orphan children could come; the others would be with relatives.

Finally, old Mr. Higgins called and as predicted, he was grumpy as an old scrooge.

"I suppose you want money!" he demanded to know.

"Not at all, Sir," Josh replied. "But if you want to donate in Jesus' name, we won't deny you your pleasure."

"Humph!" was the only reply as he hung up the receiver. But he would come.

Once they knew who all were coming, they took their old Christmas carol book down to the library and photocopied the carols they planned to sing, so each of their guests could have a copy, and so they could pass some out at each place they visited. Sam duly painted each one.

The children looked over their final needs and had a wonderful time shopping. They bought clothing for the adults on the list and food for the families. Then they gift wrapped them all with name tags and filled the large sacks. Elizabeth had drawn Christmas scenes on the sacks, which Sam filled in with his paints. Then Elizabeth labeled each with addresses. Inside each, besides clothing, toys and grocery food, were the homebaked mince pies, and most were topped with fresh Christmas wreaths. Some, however, had extra toppings of wonderfully elaborate hand-sewn baby coverlets, all decorated with ribbons and lace, or charming baby quilts, pieced together expertly by machine (on such short notice).

At 2:00 P.M. on Christmas Day, Sam stood at the door, greeting each guest with a blue, yellow, or white carnation. Most admired the nativity crèche spread below the tree before gravitating to the piano, joining in the singing as Mum sat playing carols.

All but Mr. Higgins, whose only comment was his traditional "Humph!" as he sank into a wing chair, watching warily.

Elizabeth and Josh said their quick "hellos" before putting the finishing touches on the Christmas Dinner. The table was festively set with a giant white-frosted birthday cake as the centerpiece. Yellow candles spelled out "2000" and blue script letters stated "Happy Birthday, Jesus!"

Pastor John asked the blessing with particular thanks for the wondrous gift of love in Christ Jesus. Then Father carved and passed the Christmas goose, along with the many delicacies traditional for the holidays, as well as sausages, bacon, Brussels sprouts, and roasted potatoes. The children from the Home nudged each other, smiled often, and ate heartily.

There was a wonderful feeling around the table, as if a blanket of love hung over them all. Smiles never left the widows' faces, and old Mr. Higgins was even seen to lose his scowl. Everyone remained seated while the children cleared the table.

Then, as Elizabeth lit the candles, Josh and Sam led the entire group in singing "Happy Birthday to Jesus." The widow ladies served the cake with generous portions of ice cream, much to the special delight of the children from the Home.

The mincemeat pies and plum pudding were saved for after the day's activities.

When everyone was quite finished, Pastor John rose and asked for volunteers by hands raised for the activities of the afternoon, which he read off one by one:

"First, who would like to spend time visiting inmates in the County Jail?" Father volunteered, along with two of the orphan children, to sing carols. Widow Jones said she could sing with them, too, and even read some Christmas Scriptures beforehand.

"Secondly, who would care to spend some time visiting patients in the hospital?" Mum and more children from the Home volunteered to make the rounds of the wards, singing carols and chatting with the patients.

"Third, we need volunteers for the nursing home." To

everyone's astonishment, Mr. Higgins raised his arm. "But I'll need some carolers," he growled. Two boys from the home agreed to accompany him there.

"That leaves Elizabeth, Josh, Sam, and widow Bowers to help me deliver our sacks. What do you say we all bundle up, pile into the van, and I'll drop off the jail, hospital, and nursing home people first. Then we'll deliver the sacks and go back to pick you all up. Agreed?"

"One more thing," and the pastor smiled as he brought this up. I have three Father Christmas suits. "Who will wear them?"

"Who will they fit?" asked old Mr. Higgins, finally getting into the spirit of the occasion.

"They are all fairly slender, you know," winked the plump pastor. It was soon found out that they would fit only Mr. Higgins, Father, and, of all people, Josh!

There was a happy chorus of approval and soon they were properly attired and everyone was muffled up and off.

Elizabeth turned in her seat in the front of the bus and began singing "Joy to the World," while everybody joined in. She noticed Mr. Higgins on the back seat with an orphan child on each side. He was actually singing and smiling at first one and then the other.

When the groups were all dropped off, Mrs. Bowers could hardly wait to drop off the first sack topped with one of the lacy baby coverlets she had sewn. She and Josh dressed as Father Christmas sauntered casually up to the front door, listened a moment to the sound of children inside, then deposited the sack on the top step, rang the doorbell, and ran to the van. As they pulled away, she looked back to see a thin, frail woman pick up the coverlet and look both ways—her mouth open in awe.

Years later, each and everyone who attended that birthday party for Baby Jesus recalled it clearly and fondly. Actually, its consequences were far reaching, although no one will ever know them all, just as one cannot see through the thin walls of the house where the woman opened the door to the surprise sack topped by an exquisite baby coverlet.

But a few results can be noted. For example, Mr. Higgins adopted the two orphan boys who accompanied him to the nursing home where he found his aged brother, whom he also took home to share his house on top of the hill. And his personality so softened that he actually courted the two widow ladies, and one became his bride.

The other adopted a charming girl from the Home who brought her happiness all the rest of her days.

At the jail, only the lonely prisoner knew what happened in his own life that day. He saw his son, smiling and singing about the love of Jesus. The son thought that he was dead, as the father wanted it that way rather than know the kind of life he lived. But that prisoner knew from the child's pictures, that that was, indeed his own son, and he wept for joy at the knowing.

And at the hospital, more than one patient, weary to death of the unrelenting pain and hopelessness of their situations, had given up and was in the deepest despair. But when the group entered their rooms, actually sat down and chatted awhile, read the Scripture about "God so loving the world that He gave His only begotten Son," and then when they heard the lovely singing about "What Child is this . . . ?" their hope was renewed.

It should go without saying that Jesus' Birthday Party became an annual event at #7 Park Place, and in a number of other homes down through the years.

However, there were complications. How can one attend several birthday parties at one time? So, in this particular village, which has become known as "The Jesus' Birthday Party Village," one can find invitations to such parties every day for the entire month of December.

*In him was life,*
*and that life was the light of men.*
*The light shines in the darkness;*
*but the darkness has not understood.*
*The Word became flesh and made his dwelling*
    *among us.*
*We have seen his glory, the glory of the One and Only,*
*who came from the Father, full of grace and truth.*
                            —John 1:4, 14

# Acknowledgments

Some of the works contained herein have appeared previously in other publications and are included here by permission:

From *Messenger of St. Anthony* (Padua): "Out of Egypt I Called My Son" (January, 1995), "A Wonderful Christmas" (December, 1993), "The Crimson Christmas Ribbon" (December, 1993), "The Petticoat of Heaven" (December, 1992), "Wallpaper World" (February, 1990), "Listen! Christmas Angels" (December, 1989), "Stranded in a Snowstorm" (December, 1988).

From *Celebrate Life* (2nd rights): "The Crimson Christmas Ribbon" (December, 1997).

From *Catholic Twin Circle*: "Eduardo's Homecoming" (1986).

From *The Wesleyan Advocate*: "lamb of the Lamb" (1986)

From *Nazareth Journal* (Canada, 2nd rights): "lamb of the Lamb" (Advent, 1995)

From *Companion* (Canada): "Legend of the Holly" (December, 1992), "Little Jesus" (December, 1996), "Legend of the Star-of-Bethlehem" (December, 1988).

The above-mentioned poems, "Legend of the Holly," "lamb of the Lamb," and "Little Jesus" were also published in the book *Advent Anticipations: Drawing Nearer to the Christ Child* (Nova Science Publishers, Commack, NY, 1999).